DANIELE LUZZO

THE OUTBREAK OF

CORONAVIRUS DISEASE 2019

a psychological perspective

Print ISBN: 978-1-66782-878-7
eBook ISBN: 978-1-66782-879-4

La psicologia è come il capitalismo e la democrazia. Non è che funzionino, è che non abbiamo nulla di meglio.

Psychology is like capitalism and democracy. It does not work accurately, but we have nothing better.

ABSTRACT

THIS STUDY AIMED TO EVALUATE the impact of mental health on the general population and stakeholders, and how the psychological factors have important consequences in creating public health rules. We used literature created before the pandemic and research developed during the outbreak. Additionally, we completed this review with an analysis of individual interviews and observations from welfare policies and managerial practices during the epidemic.

The 2019 pandemic has been not only a biological pandemic but also a psychological–cultural pandemic.

We found that cognitive elements are essential in the creation of public health procedures (to prevent unconscious cognitive biases or to anticipate reactions from the community). Following our assessment, the expert in the mental health fields and/or in social science should be included in the committee and decision-making group, both at the national and local levels.

Note: This work was prepared in the period March 2020–February 2021. All facts and figures refer to that timeframe.

TABLE OF CONTENTS

ACKNOWLEDGEMENTS

I WOULD LIKE TO EXTEND my gratitude to the University Uninettuno and especially to Prof Kyriakos Kouveliotis for allowing me the possibility to increase my knowledge and for offering their support during my studies and my research project.

A special thanks also to Moussa Ba, Chief of CISMU, for his stimulus to improve my career through continuous education; to Dr Christophe Bernard, Medical Chief OECD, for the economic support of this project; to Arthur Minsat for his friendship and knowledge; and finally, to Francesco Orabona for the suggested technique.

My heartfelt gratitude to Mike Knudsen, as without his support and friendship, this work would not have been possible.

Disclaimer: The views expressed herein are those of the author and do not necessarily reflect the views of the United Nations.

INTRODUCTION

THE 2020 PANDEMIC HAS BEEN not only a biological pandemic but also a psychological–cultural pandemic. Psychological, sociological and anthropological factors played a significant role in the virus's circulation.

What are the mental aspects in action during the COVID-19 outbreak and how could these components have influenced the diffusion of the infection and the public health decisions in the present and in the future?

The new coronavirus disease (SARS-CoV-2), widely known as COVID-19, was initially reported in Wuhan, China (Li et al., 2020). By September 29, 2020, it had infected 33.384 million people worldwide, killing more than 1 million individuals (source Johns Hopkins online database). The highly contagious virus (Paules, Marston and Fauci, 2020) forced a historic lockdown, in which a third of the world's population was confined at home, an unprecedented public-health tool enacted to weaken the outbreak diffusion and to let the medical and social systems adapt in confronting this contemporary challenge.

It was the first time in history that such a large part of humanity was enforced to reduce mobility that was not related to a state of war or civil unrest.

Although different nations adopted shorter or longer lockdowns, every community had to enforce movement restrictions through public repression (payment of fine or police control) because there was a general lack of will to follow these emergency public-health measures (despite evidence that these governmental decisions helped to slow down the virus diffusion) (Bonardi et al., 2020).

The psychological burden placed on the population might be huge, not to mention the resulting direct economic complications that also denote psychological stress, such as people's fear of being let go from their jobs' (Kim and Zhao, 2020).

Brooks (Brooks et al., 2020) reported an array of stressors during previous quarantine (Ebola, H1N1, SARS, Equine influence, Middle East respiratory syndrome). Across ten countries, stressors that affected the psychic well-being were noticed. Therefore, we will analyse these factors and their potential effects on the cognitive functions, the emotional spectrum, the physical consequences for the organism and the behavioural changes. These stressors increase the risk for psychiatric disorders, thereby decreasing mental health fitness.

In consideration of the above-mentioned elements, the United Nations raises awareness of the impending mental health crisis that could originate from the COVID-19 pandemic (United Nations, 2020).

Our work aims to understand the psychological implications on population and leaders, in correlation with the ongoing outbreak. We oriented our work in both the area of predictive psychology and reactive psychology. Predictive psychology refers to that set of knowledge that could describe future human behaviour (both individually and socially), basing the probabilistic analysis on evidence-based research of past actions in a similar situation. Reactive psychology refers to the support that could be needed when an adverse psychological event occurs (i.e., traumatic events).

Consequently, we will examine elements that could have delayed an appropriate response to the crisis and which long-lasting mental consequences the outbreak would produce. Understanding which vital psychological factors contributed to the diffusion of COVID-19 is useful from an organisational point of view because it offers the possibility to learn from experience and generate enough data to create better managerial procedures and policies.

In the first part, we will analyse the literature on cognitive biases, crowd management and post-traumatic stress after a major crisis.

Cognitive biases affect the decision-making process and introduce errors in the elaboration of information (Haselton, Nettle and Andrews, 2015), increasing the emotional reactions to incertitude to determine our behaviour. In a globalised world, the consequences of wide-scale events are affecting all the population at large, contributing to the spread of anxiety and rumours, impacting economic markets and overwhelming care facilities. These devastating consequences are amplified by our cognitive biases.

In the present dissertation, we analyse some cognitive biases that helped to the diffusion of SARS-CoV-2 (primarily known as COVID-19) pandemic such as Confirmation bias, Normalcy bias, Peltzman effect, Dunning–Kruger effect and Anchoring, among others.

In the second chapter, we focus on the literature generated during the COVID-19 pandemic, concentrating on the long-lasting repercussions on the population's well-being with particular attention to the psychological factors.

The pandemic will have long-lasting consequences on the public health services, and the effects on mental health will mark the national budget. There is already evidence of persistent trauma in the population, and the stake-holder should prepare adequate resources to deal with the future increase in demand for psychiatric and psychological services, as well as for physical diseases related to a poor state of mental hygiene.

In essence, the overall goal is to demonstrate that the human race is not only a physiological organism but also a psychosocial one. During the COVID-19 pandemic, as well as during the Ebola outbreak, decisions were taken based on a biological model with an attentive eye for the political and economic consequences. Those types of resolutions were only partially effective because they were not rooted in a holistic approach. We would like to present a clear indication that there is a need to rethink the reactions to COVID-19 and organise a set of policies to provide a comprehensive health response. Experts in the fields of social sciences, such as psychology, sociology and anthropology, should play an essential role in the creation and implementation of new programmes. Their actions should represent an integrated and coordinated set of operations to predict the behaviour of populations and individuals, organising the best decision-making process. In parallel, government should encourage experts in social fields to take part actively in the public discussions on media, providing context and knowledge for the general population.

The pandemic is determinate by economics, politics, public health and social behaviour, and each one of these areas should be equally engaged to prepare and develop an efficient action plan.

However, during our collection of data, we noticed that the majority of the research is based on reactive psychology and there is no scholar who developed an analysis in which lessons learnt and best practices from past-traumatic events are used to forecast the possible psychological consequences of quarantine, limitations of freedom, closure of schools and public services and Covid-related stress. This essay aims to suggest a starting point for future investigations on a population's mental well-being during a pandemic, offering some suggestions about the decision-making process in health-crisis management.

For this work, we used secondary data from the major journals and scientific reviews (PubMed, The Lancet, OECD and Asian Journal of Psychiatry, among others). Moreover, a qualitative study is utilised to attempt a broader vision of the topic, in conjunction with a qualitative ethnographic analysis to provide knowledge in real-world observations, observing social behaviour, common belief and community structures analysed through our academic experiences. For this section, we used newspapers, media coverage, individual interviews, on-field observations and ethnographic observation.

Finally, individual interviews and observations were used to have a more comprehensive approach and integrate the literature with real-life experiences. The interviews are not structured, and they last for a minimum of 45 minutes. The randomisation of data will provide anonymity. All verbal interviews have been conducted through electronic video consultation (Skype or Zoom). Thematic and content analysis is used to gather information to obtain an in-depth understanding of participants' opinions, stimuli and emotions.

At the same time, we also discuss the methodological limitations to the generalisation of our work's data, considering that during the time this essay was prepared, the pandemic was still ongoing; thus, lab-based experiments were not possible. The literature available was still in the early phase.

Nevertheless, health-care managers and national leaders could use the present work to raise awareness and advocate for a more holistic approach in the governmental health decision-making process, optimising the response to the COVID-19 outbreak and preparing the public-health system for the probability of an incoming mental health crisis. The directors could utilise the knowledge presented in our paper as technical tools to orient their decision in the budget planning for the near future, allocating appropriate assets (both in terms of material and human resources) in a timely manner.

chapter one –

LITERATURE REVIEW I

THIS CHAPTER WILL REVIEW THE literature existent before the COVID-19 pandemic and evidence the psychological factors that could have had an essential role in the ongoing outbreak.

Cognitive Biases

The goal of this paragraph is to prove how unconscious elements are affecting the decision-making process. These biases affect leaders and public-health managers in their decisions during global emergencies.

Cognitive bias creates mistakes during information-treatment analysis, also affecting the thoughts of governmental leaders. The brain has to treat external data at the highest speed in order to react promptly to environmental hazards. Considering the overwhelming collection of stimuli that reaches the senses every second, the mind has to simplify the constant influx of data; thus a series of filters, oversimplifications and overgeneralisations are automatically added to allow a rapid interpretation of the world (Wilke and Mata, 2012). Nevertheless, the increasing velocity of information flows leads to inaccuracies: stereotypes, cognitive biases, illusions, memory biases and fallacies are the price to pay for processing the signals seamlessly (Pronin, 2007). Especially during a crisis, the cognitive system privileges speed to accuracy, and the imprecision in interpreting reality has a limited effect on our chance of survival. There are possibly thousands of cognitive biases, and scholars have raised awareness of how these biases affect policies, economics (Kahneman, 2014) and other aspects of our lives.

Occasionally, the impact of cognitive biases is severe.

The ongoing COVID-19 outbreak exemplifies how wrong decisions based on cognitive errors could facilitate a pandemic spreading.

These mechanisms are automatic and independent of our will. They are not affected by age, race, sex, social power or education, influencing leaders as they do the general population.

The brain has evolved via natural selection over thousands of years, and it is optimised to treat data finitely. For example, humans are not adapted to process exponential information; we think linearly (Kurzweil, 2004). Unluckily, a virus spreads exponentially, and the magnitude of the increasing numbers is overwhelming for us. We are simply not structured to perceive the progression of a pathogenic diffusion.

We present below a list of cognitive biases, and we analyse how these biases played a role during the outbreak:

Confirmation bias. SARS-CoV-2, MERS-CoV, Ebola Virus and H1N1-Swine Flu were diseases with the potential to become pandemic, but they were controlled through different processes. The confirmation bias caused the decision-makers and the general population to select the information that confirmed the previous assumptions. Interpreting the new disease in a form that validated the idea that COVID-19 was 'just flu' (please note that in this case, a denial process was also in place to downplay the seriousness of the infection) (Johnson, 2017; Nickerson, 1998).

Normalcy bias. Individuals have the firm conviction that how something functioned in the past would continue in the future, underestimating the effects of an unprecedented disaster and the likelihood of the unexpected event (Jost, Banaji and Nosek, 2004; Omer and Alon, 1994).

Agent detection. A good deal of fake news was disseminated during the first stages of the pandemic. Such news generated confusion, fear and anxiety, and it delayed the adoption of social distance and other preventive measures among the general population. The conspiracy theory was moving from a genetically created virus to an organised multinational 'Illuminati' plot in order to explain the origin of these disruptive events. To presume the intervention of an unknown external force is a cognitive bias called agent detection.

Anchoring. The tendency to anchor the sub-sequential piece of information to the first data received. Initially, the pandemic was presented as a deadly disease affecting only elderly populations. Despite further evidence of younger cases, the community had already associated the virus with old people, creating a false sense of immunity among the young population (Furnham and Boo, 2011).

Plan-continuation bias. The tendency to continue with a program that is clearly failing. Instead of accepting the reality and altering the planned course of action, decision-makers persist in the original project.

Reactance. When individuals experience a limitation of their free will, they tend to do the opposite of what the authority is requesting, regardless of their safety, utility or consequences of the action. Despite massive information and aversive sanctions against gathering in public places, many people did not respect the confinement (Dillard and Shen, 2005; Torrance and Brehm, 1968).

Peltzman Effect. When security measures are created, the person takes higher risks because of feeling safer due to the security measures. Social distancing and wearing masks and gloves, despite being positive as a mechanism, will have aversive effects in the long-term, leading to risky behaviours (Prasad and Jena, 2014)

Curse of knowledge. Epidemiologists failed to communicate effectively because this bias prevents specialists in a field from understanding the perspective of individuals with a lesser amount of information (Birch et al., 2017).

Dunning–Kruger effect. In the space of a night, every person becomes an epidemiologist and a biologist. This bias generates the error to overestimate personal abilities in a specific domain. A sensation of illusory superiority among people with low knowledge contributed to a faulty sense of security (Pennycook et al., 2017).

Neglect of probability. Probability of an event is misinterpreted or neglected in high-arousal events. There is no intuitive awareness of risks. Our mind tends to concentrate on the badness of the result, rather than on the real probability that the outcome will become a reality (Sunstein, 2003)

Optimistic bias. Wishful thinking. Overestimating the probability of a positive conclusion despite the reality of the situation (Harris and Hahn, 2011)

System-justification theory. Status quo bias. The tendency to maintain the status quo, even if it has an aversive effect. The status quo is the baseline for security, and any sudden change is perceived as a danger.

Naïve realism. The idea that we see the external world in an objective, unbiased manner (Pronin, Gilovich and Ross, 2004).

The above-mentioned index is not exhaustive. Considering the increasing discovery of cognitive biases, it would not be even possible to redact a complete list. Benson (2016) 'classified many cognitive biases into groups according to four types of decision-making problems:

- Too much information. A person perceives that there is more information available than can be processed.

- Not enough meaning. A person perceives that there is insufficient information available for decision-making.

- Need to act fast. A person perceives that they do not have enough time to process all the information available.

- <u>What should we remember.</u> A person perceives their recall of the information available is limited, requiring them to prioritise information for access.

For each type of problem, the associated cognitive biases are placed in subgroups according to common trends' (Kinsey et al., 2019).

Even if not officially recognised, this classification evidences the influence that cognitive biases have in the decision-making process. Leaders and policymakers are not aware of these errors in their judgement because cognitive biases are unconscious and universal. Still, their impact on the outcome could have severe consequences, especially during public-health crises like the COVID-19 pandemic.

Cognitive biases determine under-reaction in mass emergencies during the rapid evaluation process. 'This decision-making approach is bounded in terms of the information available, the time available, and an individual's resources to implement such information that influences which processing mechanism is adopted. To compensate for such limitations and manage the uncertainty and complexity associated with the evaluation approach, people may employ heuristics that reduce decision-making from a cognitively effortful problem-solving task requiring mental reflection to a less effortful pattern-matching process, where stored conditions and expectations are quickly scanned to identify relevant responses. During this decision-making process, cognitive biases may occur, which cause an individual to neglect or be biased towards or against certain information: this might lead to an inappropriate and/or unexpected response' (Kinsey et al., 2019). All through a crisis, people utilise heuristics (simplified and internalised decision-making processes based on previous experiences and biological settings) to complete the insufficient number of data received and reduce reaction time. These cognitive shortcuts are good enough to adapt the behaviour to the changing circumstances in a short timeframe. They increase the sense of confidence and efficacy of individuals who adopt them automatically. Nevertheless, systematic errors could be embedded in the process, and the actors are not conscious of the detrimental effects of cognitive biases. Paradoxically, the same system that allows a rapid reply during the crisis jeopardises the individual's well-being through inappropriate response due to unconscious biases.

This section offers a cautionary tale regarding the assumption that decision-making is purely rational and cognitive. The pervasiveness of these biases is thoroughly studied in many fields, and it would be appropriate to develop a research field specifically addressed to public-health management.

Crowd Behaviour

The researches of crowd behaviour in mass emergencies have improved the understanding of people's reaction in the face of crises (Drury, 2020). 'The dynamics of crowds implies major theoretical and real-world challenges. As with many other de-centralised social and biological systems, the dynamics of crowd movements are driven by nonlinear amplification loops that promote the emergence of large-scale behavioural patterns. Recent progress in modelling and simulation techniques, coupled with advances in experimental methods and live monitoring, has provided unprecedented amounts of theoretical and empirical insights into crowd movements, ranging from the emergence of "smart" patterns of self-organisation to their breakdown when deadly crowd disasters happen' (Moussaïd et al., 2016).

The social-identity approach offers a possibility to forecast individual behaviours and predict their responses. Additionally, leaders could use social psychology to move shared identity from an antagonist position to a more collaborative attitude through ad hoc public health measures (Drury and Reicher, 2018).

'Social psychology is critical to the behaviour of members of the public as immediate responders in emergencies, in three senses. First, such public behaviour is a function of group processes—norms, relationships, and social identities. Second, what the authorities and professional groups assume about the social psychology of people in emergencies shapes policy and practice in preparedness, response, and recovery. Third, these policies and practices impact upon the public's ability to act as immediate responders' (Drury et al., 2019)With these researches in mind, public health managers could use the knowledge gained in the social sciences, using crowd modelling and social-identity theories. The study offered by the scientists in this area could provide reliable technical suggestions on preventing unexpected consequences from medical actions and restrictions, particularly during a pandemic event. The academics in the social field could act as consultants in the planning of valid measures, offering a projection of national mass behaviour and forecasting citizens' reactions to public health decisions and regulations.

Psychological Consequences of Traumatic Events

'The mechanism that causes the progressive escalation of symptoms with the passage of time leading to delayed onset post-traumatic stress disorder (PTSD) involves the process of sensitisation and kindling' (McFarlane, 2010). The 2020 pandemic represents a major stressful event for a large part of the world population, signifying a sustained stressor which impacts every aspect of life. It symbolises a significant challenge, not only psychologically but also physically. McFarlane (2010) evidences a dysregulation of cortical arousal and neurohormonal abnormalities as consequences of prolonged traumatic stress. PTSD is associated with 'chronic musculoskeletal pain, hypertension, hyperlipidaemia, obesity and cardiovascular disease'. Postponed-onset post-traumatic stress disorder leads to delayed development of physical and psychological symptoms. 'The existence of this prolonged form of PTSD emphasises how a traumatic experience can apparently lie relatively dormant with an individual only to become manifest at some future point'. The literature suggests that the signs of PTSD may not be present immediately in the aftermath of a traumatic event, as the individuals have enacted positive coping strategies to react, with the immediate consequences. But, the initial success in adapting to the adverse difficulties does not guarantee eventual and ongoing immunity against PTSD.

Traumatic memories correlate positively with arousal and avoidance (McFarlane, 1992); both are essential components in the development of

PTSD. Similarly, the pandemic epitomises a continuous series of stressful elements with prolonged exposure to horrible events (loss of beloved ones, fear of death and constant vulnerability to traumatic information). This unceasing cycle of traumatisation exposes the population to a high risk of PTSD, affecting the national public health both in the physical and psychological aspects. Thus, there is the potential that the pandemic crises will lead to an overwhelming psychiatric emergency, adding another burden to countries' sanitary systems. Likewise, the disrupted homoeostasis of individuals would increase the probability of cardiovascular disease, increased blood pressure, a surge in obesity with all the comorbid disorders associated and hyperlipidaemia, which is directly correlated with arteriosclerosis. Musculoskeletal pain related to prolonged stress was analysed by McFarlane (2007).

It is unclear how the research on psycho-physiological issues in traumatic events could apply to the COVID-19 pandemic, as this is an unprecedented experience and the health crisis is still present at the moment of this dissertation. Nevertheless, it is conceivable to use previous investigation to forecast a series of probabilistic consequences.

We have to remember the definition of PTSD from DSM-V (*DIAGNOSTIC AND STATISTICAL MANUAL OF DSM-5 TM*, 2013): '

A. Exposure to actual or threatened death, serious injury or sexual violence in one (or more) of the following ways:

1. Directly experiencing the traumatic event(s).

2. Witnessing, in person, the event (s) as it occurred to others.

3. Learning that the traumatic event(s) occurred to a close family member or close friend. In cases of actual or threatened death of a family member or friend, the event(s) must have been violent or accidental.

4. Experiencing repeated or extreme exposure to aversive details of the traumatic event(s) (e.g., first responders collecting human remains; police officers repeatedly exposed to details of child abuse). Note: Criterion A4 does not apply

to exposure through electronic media, television, movies or pictures, unless this exposure is work related.

B. Presence of one (or more) of the following intrusion symptoms associated with the traumatic event(s), beginning after the traumatic event(s) occurred:

1. Recurrent, involuntary, and intrusive distressing memories of the traumatic event(s). Note: In children older than six years, repetitive play may occur in which themes or aspects of the traumatic event(s) are expressed.

2. Recurrent distressing dreams in which the content and/or affect of the dream are related to the traumatic event(s). Note: In children, there may be frightening dreams without recognisable content.

3. Dissociative reactions (e.g., flashbacks) in which the individual feels or acts as if the traumatic event(s) were recurring. (Such reactions may occur on a continuum, with the most extreme expression being a complete loss of awareness of present surroundings.) Note: In children, trauma-specific re-enactment may occur in play.

4. Intense or prolonged psychological distress at exposure to internal or external cues that symbolise or resemble an aspect of the traumatic event(s).

5. Marked physiological reactions to internal or external cues that symbolise or resemble an aspect of the traumatic event(s).

C. Persistent avoidance of stimuli associated with the traumatic event(s), beginning after the traumatic event(s) occurred, as evidenced by one or both of the following:

1. Avoidance of or efforts to avoid distressing memories, thoughts or feelings about or closely associated with the traumatic event(s).

2. Avoidance of or efforts to avoid external reminders (people, places, conversations, activities, objects, situations) that arouse distressing memories, thoughts or feelings about or closely associated with the traumatic event(s).

D. Negative alterations in cognitions and mood associated with the traumatic event(s), beginning or worsening after the traumatic event(s) occurred, as evidenced by two (or more) of the following:

1. Inability to remember an important aspect of the traumatic event(s) (typically due to dissociative amnesia, and not to other factors such as head injury, alcohol or drugs).

2. Persistent and exaggerated negative beliefs or expectations about oneself, others, or the world (e.g., "I am bad," "No one can be trusted," "The world is completely dangerous," "My whole nervous system is permanently ruined").

3. Persistent, distorted cognitions about the cause or consequences of the traumatic event(s) that lead the individual to blame himself/herself or others.

4. Persistent negative emotional state (e.g., fear, horror, anger, guilt or shame).

5. Markedly diminished interest or participation in significant activities.

6. Feelings of detachment or estrangement from others.

7. Persistent inability to experience positive emotions (e.g., inability to experience happiness, satisfaction or loving feelings).

E. Marked alterations in arousal and reactivity associated with the traumatic event(s), beginning or worsening after the traumatic event(s) occurred, as evidenced by two (or more) of the following:

1. Irritable behaviour and angry outbursts (with little or no provocation), typically expressed as verbal or physical aggression towards people or objects.

2. Reckless or self-destructive behaviour.

3. Hypervigilance.

4. Exaggerated startle response.

5. Problems with concentration.

6. Sleep disturbance (e.g., difficulty falling or staying asleep or restless sleep).

F. Duration of the disturbance (Criteria B, C, D and E) is more than 1 month.

G. The disturbance causes clinically significant distress or impairment in social, occupational, or other important areas of functioning.

H. The disturbance is not attributable to the physiological effects of a substance (e.g., medication, alcohol) or another medical condition".

It is self-evident how the set of indicators for PTSD could be evidenced in the COVID-19 pandemic. Additionally, from the psychological point of view, there is evidence of how adverse life events contribute to the causation of psychiatric illness (Paykel, 1978). There is an increased risk for depression and neuroses and for suicide attempts.

It is indeed more challenging to evaluate the long-term costs on the younger population. Even if we know that the role of childhood distress increases mood and anxiety disorders, raising the probability of depressions (Heim and Nemeroff, 2001), we could monitor the effect on the development of the 'Covid-generation' only in the next decade. It is evidence that the generations born between the years 2015 and 2020 have been experiencing a severe change in society, with an increased level of fear among adults and communities, continuous uncertainty and an unstable and dangerous global environment.

Of course, the response of caregivers to COVID-19 stress determines the outcome for the children. 'Demonstrating resilience increases parents' self-efficacy because they are able to see evidence of both their ability to face challenges competently and to make wise choices about addressing challenges. Furthermore, parental resilience has a positive effect on the parent, the offspring and the parent–child relationship. By managing stressors, begetters feel better and can provide more nurturing attention to their minor, which enables their child to form a secure emotional attachment. Receiving nurturing attention and developing a reliable emotional attachment with parents, in turn, fosters the development of resilience in children when they experience stress' (Five Protective Factors | cfsslo, 2021).

Childhood is an ideal moment in life to develop resilience, defined as the competence to adapt to a challenging environment, an ability to respond with effective coping strategies to hardship. It implies successful adaptation when challenged by stressful life events (Bonanno, 2004; Bonanno and Diminich, 2013; Cherry et al., 2018). Resilience is 'an unusual or marked capacity to recover from or successfully cope with significant stresses, of both internal and external origin' (Werner and Smith, 1992; Werner, 1993, 2014).

Surely, there are many protective factors that could reduce the stressor's influence during the pandemic, particularly social support. Bluestone (1998) defines social support as the feeling of belonging to a social network that offers mutual support and the care or assistance that an individual perceives is received from others.

Cherry et al. (2018) indicated spiritual support, humour and laughter as protective factors in post-traumatic events, such as the Fukushima disaster, hurricane Harvey and Rana Plaza factory collapsing. Notably, 'Laughter has shown to decrease levels of cortisol, dopamine, epinephrine and growth hormone, all biomolecules related to stress hormone response. By decreasing levels of cortisol produced during chronic stress, there are fewer physiological consequences".

PROTECTIVE FACTORS	
Appropriate diet	Regular physical activity
Availability of mental health services	Religious community
Emotional competence	Strong attachments (parent–child)
Expressing gratitude	Strong social network
Genetic factors	Supportive family
Meditation and breathing exercises	Supportive peers
Parental resilience	Use of grounding techniques
Pet therapy	Volunteering

Conclusion

In this first chapter, we analysed three components related to the psychological field that could lead to better health-crisis management: cognitive biases, crowd behaviour and psychological consequences of traumatic events. Still, other elements based on social science knowledge could provide a broader vision for leaders. Culture creates the societal normative to which each member has to adhere in order to be integrated and shapes the reaction of individuals to policy and governmental decisions.

It is possible to utilise the present observations on brain functions and human and social behaviour to predict people's attitudes during a pandemic emergency. This kind of predictive psychology will help public-health managers to foster a holistic design for future policies. Besides, many assets in the field of mental health should be prepared with enough anticipation (i.e., the education process to prepare a specialist in the psychiatric domain requires at least seven years of formal university studies and on-field practices) avoiding the risk of a shortage of resources when the need arises.

In conclusion, we should remind that this chapter's limitations are associated with the impossibility to understand the psychological after-effects of the ongoing pandemic as the COVID-19 crisis is still enduring. The post-traumatic effects on adults and younger generations will produce some data in the following five years. The consequences on the adulthood behaviour of the present "'Covid-generation' will require at least ten years. Nonetheless, considering the time needed to allocate the proper resources, relevant actions should already be in progress to avoid a future crisis.

It is the leaders' role to prepare the strategy for forthcoming generations and develop the tactics to reach the ultimate goal of protecting public health, ensuring that well-being capital is preserved during the time.

chapter two –

LITERATURE REVIEW II

THIS CHAPTER WILL ANALYSE THE psychosocial-related literature created during the outbreak (the year 2020). An increasing number of researchers focused on populations' behaviour, the long-lasting impact of the pandemic and the effects of public-health preventive measures on population mental-health fitness.

Current research on psychological consequences of COVID-19

The pandemic represents a severe threat to the population's physical and mental health (Gao et al., 2020; Kang et al., 2020).

Considering the recentness of the outbreak and the ongoing fluid and dynamic situation, the usual methods to gather data for research (survey data or health insurance claims by nation information) are not available. To overcome these difficulties, Brodeur et al. (2020) and Kim and Zhao (2020) used world-browse recurrence in a well-known search engine (Google and Baidu) to obtain frequency data on words related to mental health well-being. The key words used for these researches were depression, scared, fear, anxiety, stress, nervousness, fatigue, self-harm and suicide. There was a substantial rise in the search index of these words compared to the previous year: depression increased by 225%, scared by 235%, fear by 216%, anxiety by 371%, stress by 335%, nervous by 92%, self-harm by 139% and suicide by

203% (Kim and Zhao, 2020). Brodeur et al. (2020) concluded: 'Our findings indicate that people's mental health may have been severely affected by the lockdown. There is a substantial increase in the search intensity for boredom, at two times the standard deviation in Europe and over one standard deviation in the US. We also find a significant surge in searches for loneliness, worry and sadness: these estimated coefficients are over one half of a standard deviation in Europe, but lower in the US'.

Young adults and adolescents have shown low respect for public-health actions to prevent the diffusion of COVID-19 (Geller and Warner, 1997; Yeager, Dahl and Dweck, 2018; Barari et al., 2020; Schwartz et al., 2020).

A longitudinal cohort study reported that young women conformed better to public health measures against COVID-19. The research aimed to identify the psychological components that increased the risk of noncompliance, leading young men from Switzerland to comply poorly with the public-health rules implemented to prevent pandemic diffusion. This survey involved 737 young adults of age 22. Antecedent sociodemographic, social and psychological factors were measured at ages 15 through 20. The results suggested a correlation between 'antisocial potential' and noncompliance: low acceptance of moral rules, mistrust in government, legal cynicism and poor self-control were the most relevant elements that were observed.

The modification in school management also had a significant impact on children and youths. Gruber et al. (2020) found that sleep behaviour improved thanks to changing start times. As consequences of online school starting at 10:00 a.m., there was an amelioration of sleep quality, with lower daytime sleepiness and reduced stress among adolescents. Many students woke up naturally and reported less fatigue. The pandemic forced a societal change that was beneficial for the circadian rhythm of minors.

Sleep quality is associated with the quality of mental and physical well-being and helps increase the effectiveness of treatment in Covi-19 patients, boosting their immune system (Yang et al., 2020).

The public-policy measures adopted to contain the diffusion of the pandemic had a detrimental effect on family happiness, and the magnitude of such interference in regular day-care was so high that Huebener describes the phenomena as 'disruptive exogenous shock'. In their research paper, the authors noted the challenges posed by additional at-home childcare or dependent siblings. These different pressures in the family nucleus were not evenly distributed: women and low-incoming social classes had a magnified negative impact. Women had to tolerate the highest workload, with an increased risk of reducing working hours to keep up with the children's education at home, thus leading to decreased economic power and heightened job insecurity. Furthermore, greater family stress leads to an augmentation of domestic violence. Children from lower social levels suffered the worst consequences of home education in relation to the cultural group of parents, with a reduced capability to acquire all the technological means to follow the online teaching. This difference in schooling capacity increased the tensions and stress among household members. The public policy to close day care and schools in order to slow down the pandemic had an adverse effect on educational accomplishments in low-income social groups. The studies reported 'life satisfaction declines by between 0.16 and 0.26 standard deviations (depending on the age of the youngest kid) relative to individuals without children' (Huebener et al., 2020). A descriptive analysis compared well-being during the pandemic with welfare previous to the diffusion of COVID-19 among various subgroups. They used the COMPASS survey to measure life satisfaction during the outbreak and the German Socio-Economic Panel (SOEP) as inventory for the well-being in pre-COVID-19 times. They also added a variation in different research designs to evaluate the family's differential effects with children during the pre- and post-outbreak, using adults without offspring as a control group. The idea behind this was that the eudemonia of parents with children would have followed the same trend as the control group. Their findings evidenced that school closure decreased the family's life satisfaction in nucleus composed of parents and children (especially in mothers).

This study is also particularly interesting for two other aspects: 1) the role of grandparents and 2) the social-policy measures to increase the maternal workforce. Grandparents are often the secondary childcare support in the family (after the parents). Still, due to the pandemic's specificity and the higher mortality ratio in older people, grandparents had to abandon their secondary role in the domestic duty to protect themselves.

In developed countries, there is a continuous increase effort in social policies to offer gender parity on the workforce. The primary strategy in these programs is the funding of a day-care centre, allowing the mothers to maintain their jobs even after a new child is born. The expansion of kindergarten facilities, all-day schooling, after-school programs, physical or artistic activities and care clubs strengthened the working mothers' freedom. Closing all of these activities for the pandemic would negate all the efforts of the social guidelines. In this case, public-health policies and societal programmes are antithetic and not compatible.

This public-health decision is somehow acceptable in the emergency when prompt actions are required, and the life of citizens has to be protected. In emergencies, public-health policies should prevail. However, it is not a situation that could continue for an indefinite amount of time, and it has to be used only as 'extrema ratio'.

Summarising, 'The satisfaction with life overall, with family life, and with day care decreased under COVID-19 far more for individuals with children than other individuals' (Huebener et al., 2020). The findings showed a relevant decrease in well-being for lower secondary-schooling studies, for families with children under eleven years old and for women.

'As reported in a recent survey administered during the COVID-19 pandemic, children and young adults are particularly at risk of developing anxious symptoms (Orgilés et al., 2020). The research involved a sample of 1,143 parents of Italian and Spanish children (range 3 to 18). In general, parents observed emotional and behavioural changes in their children during the quarantine: symptoms related to difficulty concentrating (76.6%), boredom

(52%), irritability (39%), restlessness (38.8%), nervousness (38%), sense of loneliness (31.3%), uneasiness (30.4%) and worries (30.1%). From the comparison between the two groups—Spanish and Italian parents—it emerged that the Italian parents reported more symptoms in their children than the Spanish parents. Further data collected on a sample of college students at the time of the spread of the epidemic in China showed how anxiety levels in young adults are mediated by certain protective factors, such as living in urban areas, the economic stability of the family and cohabitation with parents' (Saladino, Algeri and Auriemma, 2020).

Young adults and children are in risk categories that need special attention from public-health managers. Another precarious category is composed of the first respondent and physicians dealing with COVID-19 infected patients. These professionals are at high risk of contagion and possible mortality. 'The countries with the most reported physician deaths were Italy (121/278; 44%), Iran (43/278; 15%), Philippines (21/278; 8%), Indonesia (17/278; 6%), China (16/278; 6%), Spain (12/278; 4%), USA (12/278; 4%) and the UK (11/278; 4%). Ninety percent (175/194) of the deceased physicians were male. General practitioners and emergency-room doctors (78/254), respirologists (5/254), internal-medicine specialists (11/254) and anaesthesiologists (6/254) comprised 52% of those dying. Two percent of the deceased were epidemiologists (4/254), 2% were infectious disease specialists (4/254), 4% were ENTs (8/254), 4% were ophthalmologists (7/254) and 5% were dentists (9/254)' (Ing et al., 2020). Two-hundred-seventy-eight physicians died because of COVID-19, but this number is probably an underrepresentation of the real figure.

The increased mortality ratio in the therapeutic professions, fear of diffusing the virus to beloved ones, unbearable workload and media and political pressure are predictive elements for burnout. The public-health managers should take into account the effort of health-care practitioners and prepare adequate planning to assure business continuity in the medical environment. (Salvatori, 2020)

Fitting equipment should also be accounted as a means to preserve physician life, as lack of personal protective materials is often mentioned as the primary cause of death among health-care professionals. (Cibrian-Llanderal, Melgarejo-Gutierrez and Hernandez-Baltazar, 2018)

Everyone has their own unique response to the stress generated by the pandemic. There is a need for proper investigation and support to understand better the long-lasting psychosocial consequences of prolonged exposure to high arousal during the COVID-19 outbreak. Public-health managers should obtain technical advice from scholars and use the above-mentioned research to craft policies adopted to prevent and react in case of a significant mental-health crisis in societies.

Conclusion

This chapter analysed the current documentation related to psychological implication for the COVID-19 pandemic. There are rising numbers of articles, but the research in this field is still new. More studies are necessary to obtain a clear vision of the psychological consequences of the current health crisis. Despite the increasing number of papers, no relevant documentation was found about psychosocial elements contributing to the diffusion of COVID-19 virus. The scholars seem more focused on a reactive approach to the crisis in lieu of a more proactive attitude. The empirical investigations could have been more concerned with forecasting critical events or behaviour because such forecasts could act as a useful technical tool for health-care decision-makers that could use previsions on behaviours or mental illness to plan adequate interventions.

Additionally, it seems that there is a lack of correlations with the previous epidemics (i.e., Ebola) with no meta-analysis of common psychological elements among the last health crisis. From an organisational perspective, this poverty of historical data from social scientists represents a weakness in establishing policies based on lessons learnt and best practices.

From our perception, it seems that the previous pandemics (potential or real) were recorded only from an epidemiological outlook. All the experience related to governance and psychosocial behaviour is lost, forcing public-health managers to restart from scratch. It would be appropriate that the COVID-19 could teach some lessons in managing the sanitary crisis, also considering that the probability of a new pandemic in the near future is high due to globalisation and a consumerist approach.

chapter three –

METHODOLOGY

IN THIS CHAPTER, WE WILL discuss the methods used to prepare for the present work. The final goal of this dissertation was to understand the importance of psychological factors during the COVID-19 pandemic and how these elements should be accounted in the public-health measures in order to increase the efficacy of policies and improve the overall evaluation mechanisms. This document is an explorative journey in an under-researched topic during the public-health decision-making process during a health crisis. It is essential to point out that this project was developed during an ongoing crisis. The methodology and research materials had to be adapted to the environmental constraints and the available data published. There were also some ethical considerations to be addressed, particularly during individual interviews. Considering the presence of continuous stress among the population due to coronavirus's pervasive effect, asking inquiries related to the pandemic-posed ethical concerns about re-traumatisation. Research has disapproved the debriefing models after a mass emergency because it could be potentially harmful, pushing the survivors to re-experience traumatic memories. In consideration of this ethical risk, we elected to have a brief set of questions, reducing the risk of negative feelings to the minimum.

Data were gathered through relevant literature:

SOURCE	NATION
Cesifo	German
The Institute of Economic Research	Korea
Asian Journal of Psychiatry	Netherlands
Biological Psychiatry	Netherlands
Cognition	Netherlands
Fire Technology	Netherlands
Journal of Affective Disorders	Netherlands
Journal of Risk and Uncertainty	Netherlands
Journal of Socio-Economics	Netherlands
Sleep Medicine	Netherlands
Trends in Cognitive Sciences	Netherlands
Best Practice and Research: Clinical Rheumatology	United Kingdom
Cambridge University Press	United Kingdom
Communication Monographs	United Kingdom
Current Opinion in Psychology	United Kingdom
Encyclopedia of Human Behavior	United Kingdom
Journal of Affective Disorders	United Kingdom
Journal of Nursing Scholarship	United Kingdom
Neuroscience and Biobehavioral Reviews	United Kingdom
Political Psychology	United Kingdom
Psychological Medicine	United Kingdom
The Lancet	United Kingdom
The Lancet Psychiatry	United Kingdom
American Journal of Community Psychology	United States
American Psychologist	United States
Annals of the New York Academy of Sciences	United States
Brain, Behavior, and Immunity	United States

Diagnostic and Statistical Manual of Dsm-5	United States
Emerging Infectious Diseases. Centers for Disease Control and Prevention (CDC)	United States
JAMA—Journal of the American Medical Association.	United States
Journal of Child Psychology and Psychiatry	United States
Journal of Nervous and Mental Disease	United States
Journal of Nursing Scholarship	United States
MedRxiv	United States
MMWR—Morbidity and Mortality Weekly Report	United States
New England Journal of Medicine	United States
Nursing Outlook	United States
Perspectives on Psychological Science	United States
PLoS ONE	United States
Psychiatric Services	United States
Psychological Bulletin	United States
Psychological Review	United States
Psychological Review	United States
Psychonomic Bulletin and Review	United States
Review of General Psychology	United States
Science Direct	United States
Sleep Medicine	United States
The American Journal of Psychology	United States
The Handbook of Evolutionary Psychology	United States
World Psychiatry	United States

The information gathered through literature was divided into two areas:

1) Research conducted before the virus outbreak.

2) Research prepared during the virus outbreak.

The articles were selected based on the importance of the journals where they were published and relevance to the following themes: Psychological traits that impact decisional processes through mass emergencies, social–psychological aspects in crowd behaviour in public crises, post-traumatic psychological implication, the psychic effects related to quarantine, affected well-being in target population during COVID-19 outbreak and mental-health consequences after shocking events.

A series of interviews were conducted among volunteer attendees to complete the literature with the specific purpose to provide a broader view of the psychological aspects of the current crisis. This is a non-probability sampling method that had the goal to develop an initial understanding, offering fresh approaches to appreciate the formerly mentioned literature. In particular, the subjects that contributed to the examinations were snowball samples, in which the previous participants recruited other volunteers.

Data were collected through a semi-structured interview via video consultations (Skype, WhatsApp, Zoom), 98 individuals took part in the evaluation (48 male, 50 female), and the age range was 30 to 50. They had a tertiary education and worked in middle-high jobs. Sixty percent were married and 40% were singles. Seventy-three percent lived in a different country from their relatives. All came from an international background.

The key interview questions were: (1) How did you feel during the coronavirus epidemic? (2) What were your emotions during the outbreak? (3) What do you think about the current pandemic? (4) What aspects of the pandemic were more difficult to manage for you? (5) Do you have any other thoughts that you would like to share?

The sessions lasted a minimum of forty-five minutes. The participants appreciated the interview as a means to vent out unpleasant feelings.

The essential elements of the encounters were transcribed, and textual analysis was conducted. A deductive approach to the thematic investigation was utilised based on the previous literature. Particularly, it was relevant to the theoretical framework offered by the initial screening of pertinent documentation that represented the basis for a latent evaluation of the collected questionings.

The interviews were coded following recurring themes: psychological distress, physical consequences related to stress, psychiatric disorders, cognitive impairment and emotional impact.

Fear of transmitting the contagion to beloved ones was high: 'I would like to be near my parents as they are old, but I cannot bear the idea to infect them. I am struggling between my desire to be with them and my fear to contaminate them with the virus'.

Work-related consequences were also relevant: 'I am scared to lose my job if I became sick, in case I will be sick. I am thinking to hide the fact that I am unwell. Maybe I could take some annual leave. Thus they will not know I was sick. It could affect my career. I know the stigma around the infection'.

Twelve participants reported invasive circular thoughts about the COVID-19: 'I cannot concentrate, I continue to think about the virus. Was it planned? What will happen to my family? Did I have to prepare for the funeral for my father? I continue to look for information. I cannot even sleep properly'.

Among individuals without a partner, loneliness was a recurring theme: 'I feel so lonely. Before the outbreak I had a rich social life, friends, theatre, cinema and now I spend all my time on the computer and I am scared to meet anyone. I would like someone to share the solitude and the difficulties'.

Two people expressed an 'excessive use of computers, screens and digital technologies'.

In the group, only one subject lost a relative due to the COVID-19, and she reported: 'I am feeling so guilty. I cannot even attend the funeral of my father. Really, I tried everything, but the borders were closed. I cannot travel, and I cannot say a proper farewell to him. I am ashamed to be his daughter, he was good with me, and I could not even be there for him'.

Rage against the government and social institutions was recorded: 'Why [leader] did not react before? It's always a question of money and power. They don't care about us, it's just another occasion to gain political power'. The miscommunication from national institutions was also a source of anger and anxiety: 'They said the masks are not useful, then made a law to oblige you to wear it. They have no idea what they are doing. You have to stay at home, but the economy should run. They are liars, incompetents'.

Denial and diverting attention were the primary coping strategies 'Well, I try not to think about it. I listen to music, play PlayStation, watch a lot of Netflix series. What should I have to do? I cannot become crazy about this'.

Only five of interviewed looked for mental-health support.

The size of the sample was limited by the constraints of reaching a higher number of people, also because there was resistance to participate in the interview. Participants were eager to vent, but not to reply to a semi-structured interview showed a willingness to share their perceptions of the event but not to recall specific emotions or feelings related to the pandemic. A probable hypothesis for this reticence is that they experienced the recalling of memories too painful. A reaction of avoidance is possible during high-stress life events, and the request to focus on unpleasant memories could be perceived as aggressive, even as a re-traumatisation.

The snowball method utilised had the side-effect to increase the homogeneity of the studied group (i.e., the individuals who were recruited for the interview presented similar level of education, household income and international status), increasing the risk of limited validity to a specific sub-group. Nevertheless, the sample investigated offered interesting research ideas and suggestions that were further analysed through the literature review.

For the analysis on the impact of schools' closure on family well-being, the findings were based on two sources: COMPASS survey data and German-Socio-Economic-Panel (Huebener et al., 2020).

The first data set was based on 14.781 interviews (May through July 2020) using a Likert scale ranging from 'not satisfied at all' (0 points) to 'very satisfied' (10 points). They identified the parents with dependent children, focusing on the households in which a child younger than sixteen years lived.

At the opposite, the adult households without a child under sixteen years were identified as individuals without dependents.

The second data set was a subset of the 2018 SOEP (33.000 individuals) that included the same questions as the COMPASS survey. The median age was 45.6 in the SOEP sub-sample and 45.4 in the COMPASS sample.

Nevertheless, it is important to observe that the SOEP interview was conducted in person, and the COMPASS survey was an online questionnaire. This methodological choice could be a significant weakness in the study, as a direct comparison is not entirely possible. Furthermore, the two studies were submitted in different social settings (normal versus emergency), and that could also influence the answers to the reported level of life satisfaction. Saying that, this exercise is a crucial base to evidence the need for research on the consequences of public health policies.

'It would be advisable for crisis teams at regional and national levels, from the beginning of a pandemic, to include not only virologists, medical experts in general, and economists, but also representatives of family and education policy experts. It is clear from the first wave of COVID-19 that concerns for the well-being of families must not take second place to concern for the economy and other areas, because, otherwise, the human potential of today and tomorrow cannot develop optimally in the long term' (Huebener et al., 2020).

Conclusion

The above-mentioned methodology allowed the collection of information and data during the ongoing crisis, and it was adopted following the environmental constraints. The purpose of the selected method was not intended to represent the highest standard in reliability and validity, but to provide a stimulus for further study in this discipline, utilising more robust and solid research strategies in the future. The weakness in some methodological arguments is fully compensated by the original approach to the subject, offering an entry point to be used by scholars interested in psycho-sociological factors during a worldwide pandemic.

chapter four –

FINDINGS/ANALYSIS/ DISCUSSION

4.1 findings

IN THIS CHAPTER, THE FIGURES collected are presented and organised in arrays to evidence the psychological elements relevant to our topics. We show the data with aggregation in four clusters:

1) Stressors.

2) Maladaptive behaviour.

3) Consequences on physical and mental health.

4) Protective factors.

The research analyses and the interviews suggested a list of stressors commonly experienced by the population through different cultural backgrounds:

Physical	Emotional	Behavioural	Cognitive	Psychiatric
Back pain	Anger	Aggressiveness	Circular thoughts	Depression
Chest pains	Distrust	Diffusion of fake news	Denial	Anxiety disorder
Digestive problems	Emptiness or hopelessness	Drug abuse	Impaired cognitive functions	Burnout
Dizziness	Fear	Excessive attention to symptoms	Impaired executive function	CPTSD
Headaches	Guilt	Increase in psychotropic medication	Misjudgement	Paranoia
High blood pressure	Helplessness	Increased screen time	Lack of focus	Dissociative symptoms
High cholesterol	Lower self-esteem	Isolation	Loss of memory	Personality disorders
Low energy	Melancholy	Restlessness	Nightmares	PTSD
Low human immune system	Mood fluctuations	Self-harm	Rumination	
Low sex drive	Rage	Suicide	Burnout	
Sleep deprivation	Sadness	Violence	Stress	

These stressors generated a set of negative consequences on well-being. The interviews and literature observed serious psychological challenges related to: isolation due to quarantine, wearing protective equipment, difficulties in providing for basic needs, financial distress, incertitude for the future, digital overconsumption, social distancing, impossibility to reach the family, the COVID-19 disease, death of beloved ones, misinformation, over information, shortage of health care, seclusion, reduced freedom of movement, overwhelming media exposure, job insecurity.

Newall et al. (2013) found that the correlation between loneliness and mortality rate and chronic stress has a direct impact on physical well-being (Quick, 1987; Schnurr, P. P. and Green, 2005). The brain's higher functions, related to planning, organising, time management, troubleshooting, conceptualisation and decision-making, are impaired by negative emotions (Heilman et al., 2010; Shields et al., 2016). Higher functions present in the prefrontal cortex optimise the interaction with the environment through working memory, cognitive flexibility and inhibitory control (Miyake et al., 2000). These functions are affected by stress, lack of sleep, loneliness or lack of exercise (Diamond, 2013).

'The prefrontal cortex acts as a controller of executive functions. The executive functions, which help us to organise thoughts, tend to be interrupted when the stressors load is too high' (Cibrian-Llanderal, Melgarejo-Gutierrez and Hernandez-Baltazar, 2018). We have to remind that stress generates a cellular oxidative reaction as the stressor promotes the stimulation of hypothalamus to secrete adrenocorticotropic (ACTH) hormone.

'Hyperactivity of the hypothalamic-pituitary-adrenal (HPA) axis is accepted as one of the fundamental biological mechanisms that underlie major depression. This hyperactivity is caused by diminished feedback inhibition of glucocorticoids (GC)-induced reduction of HPA axis signalling and increased corticotrophin-releasing hormone (CRH) secretion from the hypothalamic paraventricular nucleus (PVN) and extra-hypothalamic neurons. During chronic stress-induced inhibition of systemic feedback, cytosolic glucocorticoid receptor (GR) levels were significantly changed in the prefrontal cortex (PFC) and hippocampus. Both structures are known to be deeply involved in the pathogenesis of depression. Cytokines secreted by both immune and non-immune cells can markedly affect neurotransmission within regulatory brain circuits related to the expression of emotions' (Gadek-Michalska et al., 2013). 'Acute stress increases the expression of cytokines and other inflammatory-related factors in the CNS, plasma and endocrine glands, and activation of inflammatory signalling pathways within the hypothalamic-pituitary-adrenal (HPA) axis may play a key role in later stress sensitisation' (Hueston and Deak, 2014).

'Human studies have revealed that the self-control of stress can promote the reduction of the action of the amygdala, and the subject can solve the stressful situation. An opposite situation will lead to a deleterious effect on mental and physical health. It has been determined that the absence of control of stress can promote the acquisition of addictive practices. During adolescence, addiction to nicotine, or even to the internet, causes cortical alterations due to decreased mesolimbic dopaminergic function' (Cibrian-Llanderal, Melgarejo-Gutierrez and Hernandez-Baltazar, 2018).

Indeed, Mesurado, Vidal and Mestre (2018) exposed 'that anger had a direct relationship with pro-social behaviour and aggression'.

'A history of a previous suicide attempt is the strongest predictor for future suicidal ideation and behaviour (SIB), including suicide ideation, suicide attempts and suicide' (Parra-Uribe et al., 2017). Young age seems to be a risk factor in a suicide attempt and reattempt. 'Early life stress…has been associated with the onset and the severity of psychiatric disorders in adults' (Carr et al., 2013), and environmental factors play a key role in the development of psychiatric illnesses (Schmitt et al., 2014). Stress imposes a reorganisation of the limbic system, and it is correlated with almost all psychopathological entities (Riboni and Belzung, 2017).

The table's component creates a retro-feedback, increasing the relevance of symptoms and mutually influencing each other in a self-sustained negative system.

It is important to remember that the major part of maladaptive behaviours (excessive attention to symptoms, diffusion of fake news, a surge in psychotropic medication, an increase of drug use, avoidance, isolation, etc.) created a vicious circuit in which the inappropriate coping mechanism generates a set of negative emotions and a diminished capacity of judgement that self-sustain the same maladaptive behaviours. Therefore, if professional help is not provided, the mental-health consequences could be severe:

depression, suicidal thought, self-harm, sleep deprivation, rumination and circular thoughts, PTSD, anxiety, nightmares, lower self-esteem, cognitively impaired functions, irritability and impaired judgement.

The strong correlation among these elements and the individual's well-being impact all aspects of life: the weakened executive functions lead to a decrease in the working capacity, the mood negative behaviour affects relations with families and friends and the psychiatric disorder requires a medicalised approach that could reduce social functionality.

Additionally, the huge level of stress and cortisol generated as a consequence of an unsupportive environment could lead to physical suffering which co-correlates with mental well-being: headache, back pain, high blood pressure, somatisation, increase in cholesterol, fatigue, weaker human immune system, digestive problems, reduced sex drive, heightened inflammation (Hänsel et al., 2010) and weakened immune function (Segerstrom and Miller, 2004).

Nevertheless, numerous protective factors were also recorded: family and social help, accurate and prompt information, medical care, psychosocial assistance, maintaining transparency on the decision-making process, humour, spiritual support, altruism, trust, peer-support programmes, aid from co-workers and line managers, household income and life-work balance.

Yang et al. (2020) revealed that, 'psychosocial symptoms had a strong positive association with several social-support factors'. Sleep quality seems to be strongly correlated with the relationship with family or friends, care from colleagues and good relations with physical and mental-health workers. It is critical to remind that sleep quality is fundamental to preserve mental-health fitness and strengthen the immune system (Irwin, 2002; Lange, Dimitrov and Born, 2010).

The above-mentioned elements played a particular role among healthcare workers and first responders (Fekih-Romdhane et al., 2020). As already noticed during other natural disasters and pandemic situations (Lehmann et al., 2015). Medical staff are under pressure with an unacceptable workload, and seven research articles explained that compared to the overall population, healthcare providers experienced a high level of insomnia, anxiety, somatisation and depression (Ahmed et al., 2020; Ren et al., 2020; Zhou et al., 2020) due to exhausting working hours, fear of contagion of their beloved ones, fatigue and constant risks of infections. Particularly, the workload led to burnout through exhaustion. The studies showed a higher danger for female clinical staff, while advanced age was a protective factor against depression, anxiety and insomnia. Level of revenue and years of experience were defensive mechanisms against suicidal risk. Further research has to be focused on the medical staff's well-being (Kang et al., 2020), mostly on medical personnel's self-destructive behaviour (Goyal et al., 2020).

Mental-health fitness depends on the interaction between stressors and protective factors in a determinate environment and in a specific cultural context. Critical elements in the prediction of mental health well-being are gender, race, age, socio-economic status, education, genetics, nature of stressors, timing and persistence of stressors (Mraek and Haggerty, 1994).

4.2 analysis

This work's main goal was to understand the COVID-19 from a psychological viewpoint, with the implicit assumptions that the public-health management of a crisis of this magnitude could benefit from a different point of observation. The collection of materials and the interviews seems to indicate the relevance of psychological factors during the outbreak. However, even psychological analysis could be experienced from divergent angles and with various objectives, considering human behaviour's complexity. In this paper, we focused our attention mainly on two areas:

1. How research in the psychological field could benefit the public-health supervision of COVID-19?

2. How health managers should prepare for the psychological consequences of the ongoing biological crisis?

The collected data suggest that psychological aspects (cognitive biases) could play a fundamental role in the public-health-governance decision-making process, affecting the resolutions adopted by leaders and/or reducing the efficacy in adopting policies, impacting the compliance and appropriate behaviour from the population. The literature evidence psychosocial elements that play a crucial aspect in providing the best leadership decisions in a mass emergency context. Superintending a sequence of critical processes during a humanitarian crisis could represent a real challenge for leaders and top managers in the medical sector. Timely interventions, urgency and impact on populations express a series of constraints that increase the pressure on the management team. Cognitive biases are embedded in the organisational process, in consideration of the omnipresent nature of these psychological mechanisms. Handling and coordinating a correct response to the emergency requires monitoring the unconscious aspects that are affecting the administrators.

Applying due diligence to COVID-19 crisis management calls for a proper understanding of the technical elements involved during supervision and coordination. The role of leaders is not only to react to the ongoing pandemic but also to foresee potential risks.

On this point, social research on crowd behaviour offers an analytical tool to understand population conduct, suggesting a way to improve the policies and/or create alternative contingency plans based on predictive behaviour valid for the major part of the community. Using mass-emergency model behaviour could predict people's actions and prepare a contingent plan to reduce difficulties.

A practical example gathered from French newspapers: The day of lockdown, there was a mass migration from the Paris region to touristic locations (i.e., Île de Ré). The sudden upsurge in the population (+30%) in small villages created a shortage of food and necessary supplies that also impacted the residents. An analysis of Parisian crowd movement could have prevented that massive exodus, and the public-health plan could have alerted local stores to increase their supply or the public-health manager could have suggested the block of national transportation from the French capital in order to reduce the number of migrants and the consequent spreading of the virus in localities less affected by the pandemic.

An additional example came from Italy: when the government announced the lockdown, a mass migration happened from the northern regions (where the disease was highly present) to the southern regions (which were almost Covid-free). This behaviour significantly increased the dispersion of COVID-19 in Italy, creating social tensions between southern and northern Italians. Similarly to the French case, utilisation of the expertise of social scientists, social psychologists and sociologists, could have suggested an improved way to manage the public health in the country. Preventive steps could have been adopted if the Italian national health management had considered a more socio-psychological approach. Some measure of protection would have contained the expansion of COVID-19 in the country, such as a ban on transportation to South Italy or a long, deterrent media campaign to raise awareness in the Italian population. Finally, even if the preventive measures had been unsuccessful because of unforeseeable factors, decisive action could have been planned to reduce the tension between the northern and the southern communities in the country.

Behaviour analysis could have predicted the increasing demand in primary goods, avoiding the disruption of the supply chain. Some essential items (toilet paper, flour, water, medical supplies, etc.) are in prime need during a mass emergency, as already recorded during the Ebola crisis.

Even more relevant is the leader's accountability for the population's future well-being. There is a moral and professional duty to train the necessary resources, plan ahead and prepare the material and human capabilities to prevent loss of quality of life.

Related to the mental-health consequences of COVID-19, the researches created during the ongoing pandemic are concordant on the considerable impact on mental health in the populations. Even if the investigations are still being produced and there is the need to collect more evidence, the WHO raised awareness about the probability of a psychiatric crisis after the biological turmoil.

The series of interviews we undertook seems to confirm the impact on the psychological well-being of the population. Anxiety, uncertainty, a great degree of stress and negative thoughts were relevant among the individuals who accepted to participate in our interview. This set of disruptive emotions generated cognitive impairment on the high executive functions present in the cerebral frontal lobe, creating difficulties in planning, organisation, focus and time management. The constant level of fear induced by an overwhelming media concentration of news on COVID-19 suggests a possible impact on physical fitness. The scholars have evidenced the increased cortisol level due to chronic stress; this high degree of cortisol is directly correlated with cardiovascular diseases.

Furthermore, the limited freedom of movement and the closing of sports centres increase the risk of obesity, adding another element for infarcts, diabetes, high blood pressure and other diseases. During the interview, a certain level of aggressiveness was noticed; this could be due to stress factors, but also could be due to physical modification in the body as a result of the current sanitary situation. Despite its origins, the suppressed rage could generate interpersonal conflicts and social tension. Eventually, these negative emotions could be exploited from extremist parties to steer the general population's consensus towards more extreme political actions.

As such, there is a question about alternative public-health measures that could prevent the need to impose self-isolation (such as social distancing, cancellation of mass gatherings and school closures). The quarantine is a strong epidemiological tool to prevent virus diffusion, but the application of reduced freedom of movement should be weighted in consideration of long-lasting psychological effects. The long-term after-effects on population well-being as a result of COVID-19 outbreak require further studies.

Nevertheless, the public-health manager has been alerted to prepare a contingency plan for the incoming mental-health crisis. Management, especially in public health, should have the capacity to anticipate the need and to propose solutions and strategies for future sanitary risks.

Policymakers may wish to invest more resources in a psychosocial analysis of approved protocols and improve such policies or adopt preventive measures. As previously discussed, school closure resulted in an increased amount of domestic violence. It would have been conceivable to raise awareness about this potential danger; thus decision-makers could have prepared an emergency plan to offer support to victims of abuse, creating ad hoc hotlines and capabilities as well as reinforcing the existing protocols. Coordination with the local police could also be strengthened, and the agents could be alerted about a possible increase in domestic violence.

Technical skills are essential instruments for executive managers. They need the knowledge and competences to implement field-specific, expert tasks. The information gathered through the cooperation with experts and consultants empowers a leader to harmonise work, anticipate problems, communicate successfully and obtain a solid grasp of the big picture. It is the responsibility of health administrators to offer a vision in the long-term and direct national resources onto the right track. In order to accomplish such a mission, they should use all the fields at their disposal, such as social scientists and professionals in the field of human behaviour.

The public health decision-makers should base their plans and course of actions on a solid experimental background. Experimenters offer the scientific knowledge and the technological advances that leaders need to organise and tailor medical-care planning and implement the corrective activities to ensure global well-being. In a globalised world, welfare problems cross national borders, as demonstrated by the recent pandemic outbreak. Consequently, the information obtained by a worldwide-designed analysis project should also provide an international perspective. A multidisciplinary and multicultural approach in research and public-health intervention is a necessity in an interconnected planet.

Nowadays, a single entity's resources are not any more adequate to evaluate the complexity of the global health system, and medical innovation results from a worldwide effort. Sharing intelligence among different stakeholders is essential in the new, globalised era.

The information has to be meaningful, timely and accurate, otherwise there is the risk that we use data that are no longer valid or relevant. Our biases could be involved (Grimes and Schulz, 2002), and we could have the tendency to choose only the knowledge pertinent to confirm our preferences (Sica, 2006), and not the ones appropriate to respond to our research question adequately.

An appropriate assessment could help managers better understand the community's health needs, measuring programmes and treatments' outcomes. Researchers could clarify the most efficient and cost-effective policies to be implemented, with the advantages and setbacks, creating a solid baseline to present motivations and purposes to the stakeholders. The data set of robust experiments on mental-health consequences during the growing crisis could lead to reinforcing the case for funding requests, informing the donors of the expected benefits of their investments. The study could be the pillar for strategic planning in the managerial vision of quality improvement, decreasing expenses and saving resources and time. Getting a stronger grasp of the complexity of the COVID-19 pandemic could be an advantage in addressing management of the national sanitary crisis. Understanding interaction between communities, expectations and perceptions could lead to a reduction of leaders' errors and higher compliance from society.

In summary, the collected information shows that social scientists should always be included in all decision-making process levels to reduce biased choices, anticipate population behaviour and forecast psychosocial consequences of final governmental decisions. The present work could offer a starting point for future scholars for the investigation of socio-psychological factors as essential tools for sound managerial judgement during mass biological emergencies.

There were some limitations in this study, considering the ongoing virus outbreak during this paper's preparation. We analysed the current documentation on the psychological-related effect of COVID-19, but there is a lack of researchers on the psychosocial elements that contributed to the diffusion of the pandemic, and there is a void in the literature on evidence-based analysis of social aspects as determinants and contributive factors for the virus spreading among the population.

On the other hand, this work had the primary goal of demonstrating the lack of social research during the decision process used by worldwide nations. This is a missing piece of the puzzle for adopting effective national health measures to diminish the circulation of COVID-19. Despite the evidence that psychological factors are essential in the prevention of virus dissemination and in the future planning strategies, no social scientist is involved in the decision-making process. Moreover, the media are entirely ignoring the socio-cultural aspect of COVID-19 diffusions, creating confusion among the population.

The fragmentation of leaders' actions is preventing a correct managerial approach to the 2020 crisis. From one side, top managers and governmental representatives lack accurate information to address the situation. On the other side, a globalised hazard cannot be solved on a social level (and some countries like Italy implemented sub-national decentralisation of interventions to avoid political turmoil). In an interconnected community, restraining the decisions to a single country has been having a detrimental effect by increasing the national social tension and decreasing population well-being. The managers should adopt a worldwide vision and a transnational approach to cope adequately with the long-term consequences in terms of both mental and physical health.

International organisations should play a pivotal role in offering a forum of discussion to harmonise the sanitary regulations, the same part that the supranational entities are playing in politics and economics. Provision of a place to discuss holistic public medical policies with globalised actions to formulate a contingency plan for a universal health crisis, adopting measures for ongoing problems and analysing long-term consequences and impact of critical health elements worldwide.

There is the hope that a new international organisation will arise from the 2020 negative experience and that an intergovernmental approach would be developed to better cope with a future worldwide health crisis, allowing the national public health to harmonise their procedures and policies in a framework of global governance.

4.3 discussion

This document supports the theory that the COVID-19 pandemic has profound psychological implications, both in the sense of crisis management and in the long-term consequences.

The hypothesis that the sanitary emergency had adverse psychological effects on the population's well-being is supported by the literature developed in the year 2020, and the research already established in the previous years. Furthermore, the interviews collected preparing this dissertation are coherent, with a significant level of distress due to the stress caused by the pandemic.

The people's quality of life (both in terms of physical and psychological well-being) has been affected by the COVID-19 crisis. The data suggest that there will be long-lasting mental health repercussions.

These findings are in line with a statement on the WHO website in which there is a call for action to increase investment in the mental-health public policies in order to avert a significant psychic meltdown.

The results should be considered when preparing a management agenda for the COVID-19 crisis (or other pandemic-related crises). There is a clear understanding of the consequences of psychic health as well as the psychological aspect influencing leadership decisions on public health. In order to have a more robust set of findings, further research should be developed to verify the correlations between psychological facets and pandemic diffusions. The supervisors must have the competence to plan, implement, monitor and control processes in order to prevent an oncoming psychiatric crisis. One of the most relevant aspects that leaders should address is the health care-professional shortage, with specific competences in the mental-health field (psychiatrist, psychiatric nurses, psychologist, neuroscientist, psychotherapist and similar experts), as well as the lack of culturally appropriate care systems. The governments' health-care leaders should adopt a long-term global vision to maximise benefits for the population in order to obtain the most efficient use of the resources. Health is an inherited durable capital good that needs proper research, analysis, and planning to reduce the depreciation over time (Grossman, 1972).

The managers have to identify population needs and plan projects that could respond to and should expect such necessities, providing an adequate supply chain in order to have the materials and human capacity to face the predicted demand. The data gathered during this work seems to indicate non-communicable, chronic diseases will increase due to the pandemic, particularly mental-health conditions.

Health managers will have the challenges to condense the information deriving from a globalised, multicultural society with an accelerated technological speed during a pandemic crisis. They have to take into account the cons and pros, depending on moral values and ethical standards of individuals.

The forthcoming specialist on the topic could use this work as a basis to develop theories and prepare an analysis that could lead to an improved understanding of the pandemic on a worldwide scale, with particular attention for the psychological aspects. This new research would help the epidemiologists offer better recommendations and the policymakers to implement more holistic policies with a broader view towards the population's well-being.

The utilisation of a proactive social-scientist approach would increase the effectiveness and will lead to a faster reaction during a pandemic-related crisis.

In summary, our study seems to support the importance of mental-health and social-science professionals to enhance both efficacy and efficiency, improving the reactions to the pandemic.

It is worth noting the parallelism between the governance of the Ebola pandemic and the COVID-19 pandemic. The same types of errors are present in the two pandemics' public-health management, and they can be summed up in a lack of clear vision due to missing data. During the Ebola virus crisis management, misconceptions and miscalculations prevented an optimised approach, converting a sanitary crisis into a cultural one. We can remember the hostility of the population towards medical practitioners, the citizens' unwillingness to comply with security measures, the diffusion of fake news, the miscommunication or inadequate communication, the lack of cultural context, the oversimplification of crowd behaviour and the absence of planning and adequate capabilities.

The 2014 Ebola outbreak in West Africa is an example of the influence of locally developed disease in a globalised world. This outbreak had a broad media impact because 11 cases of Ebola were treated in the USA (CDC website), disseminating fear but also allowing the allocation of resources and assets to treat the disease globally. It is a good precedent of a wasted opportunity. There were many lessons that could have been learnt from the Ebola crisis, but there was not a joint effort to collect that experience. The same situation that is currently being experienced with COVID-19 could have happened six years earlier. The Ebola virus was present in Africa, America and Europe, and an appropriate amount of means was allocated to prevent the rise of a global pandemic. Sadly, it seems that red alert was not recorded and no preparation was made by world or health leaders.

Until the administrators consider the pandemics from an epidemiological point of view, there will be no lessons learnt from experiences. The same errors noticed during the Ebola pandemic could have been avoided during the ongoing critical situation with a holistic approach and a social-scientist data collection from the previous health emergency. An analysis of social, psychological and anthropological consequences should have been conducted to take advantage of the current historical situation. There is no possibility to overcome this current crisis and future pandemics without integrated collaboration between epidemiology, politics, economics and social science.

The quality of care is directly related to the cultural element and to the religious beliefs adopted by the population. Misunderstandings and stereotypes could generate antagonism towards the health providers, increasing the healing reaction time and reducing the effectiveness of the health-management system. Barriers between antithetic cultures could create conflicts. Generalisations and oversimplification are risky because they could lead to errors.

A hyper-simplification of this health crisis through a biological model is a sure defeat.

The ongoing pandemic is acting as a magnifying glass on social problems: economic inequalities, inadequate mental-health support, isolation, unhealthy living conditions, societal tension, digital divide, weak and unfair academic system, unethical labour practices, ineffective international health policies, extremist political parties and highly bureaucratic decision-making processes are the challenges amplified by the medical crisis. Educational and socio-economic backgrounds are correlated with the consequences on individuals' well-being, not only because a greater position on the social ladder ensures a better quality of care but also because increased education contributes to an improved risk evaluation.

Patients are scared to visit hospitals, even if their physical condition is deteriorating (i.e., to attend chemotherapy) because they have not the competencies to appreciate the difference between certitude of health deterioration due to lack of care and the probability to be infected by COVID-19.

It is also possible that a cognitive bias about risk/reward is playing a major role. Further analysis should be conducted.

Populations and leaders alike should stop to consider the COVID-19 catastrophe as an exceptional historical event. The increasing number of individuals and the livestock that shares humanity's space, associated with the abuse of resources, multiplies the probability of spreading viruses, diseases and zoonoses.

Thus, the 2020 sanitary crisis is probably the first of a long pandemic list that humanity will have to face if the current global trend continues. The risk of a pandemic is part of a globalised world, untethered from any environmental ethics in a framework of consumerist capitalism.

The ongoing sanitary globalised emergency results from a precise business model generated by everyday consumerist culture.

The medical approach is based on a human ecological perspective, considering the relation of individual people and communities with their particular physical and social settings.

From an individual environmental viewpoint, aspects of everyday activity that directly impact healthiness are pivot points (population, environment and culture). The subjective perceptions and feelings about one's physical state (illness) are essential in the community's quality of life, despite being a subjective perception and not related to some diagnostically solved problem, perceptions and feelings about illness dramatically impact the well-being of the individual.

The present discussion should also consider the limitation of our data collection. Because of the ongoing crisis and the associated reduced mobility, it was a challenge to gather enough information due to the lack of appropriate research on this recent topic. Scholars are continuously producing new articles on the psychological impact of COVID-19 pandemic, but the long-term mental health implication will offer some relevant data in the near future. During our analysis of the result, we noticed a bias in the collection of scientific journals: there is an over-representation of Anglo-Saxon documents, as the collected publications are mainly from the UK and the US.

It is essential to remind that this work was prepared at the beginning of the medical crisis. Therefore, the generalisability of the results is limited by the size sample and the available research. The methodological choices were forced by the social situation and the reduced freedom of movement. The interviews were conducted online; thus, confounding variables are possible due to the obligation to adjust the methodology to the circumstances.

Hence, there is a need to have further data gathering and analysis that will lead to an improved decisional process with the outcome of better health for the general population. A collection of scientific data based on experience and reliable information will allow a precise, optimal allocation of resources.

Particularly challenging will be gaining reliable knowledge in developing countries and the cross-analysis between countries with different policies and divergent implemented actions against the pandemic.

Digital transformation will allow an improved data collection, and artificial intelligence could offer an exciting opportunity to discover meta-trends, improving the statistical processing and analysis. The COVID-19 crisis supported telemedicine's mass adoption and the evolution of new advanced techniques in creating a vaccine. The same effort in applying IT development to real-life problems should be adopted to promote the population's mental well-being and prepare adequate resources for future needs in the psychiatric field.

An additional limitation of our work is the impossibility of understanding the psychological impact of the economic crisis generated by the ongoing pandemic. Great efforts are currently provided to sustain the markets, but the forthcoming predictions are gloomy, at best. The COVID-19 problem is first and foremost a medical crisis, and secondly a financial turmoil that is affecting globalisation and worldwide markets. Thus, a considerable sum of money is directed to reinforce the health system while another substantial amount is spent on strengthening the monetary structure. Generally, health conditions improve with social status and the level of income. However, when the crisis is global and the entire medical apparatus is at risk of collapsing, only proper management could preserve the health systems, achieving organisational goals through planning, organising, directing and controlling human and physical resources. The COVID-19 is a severe challenge that pushes world government and business leaders to balance economy, politics, health and efficient organisation.

The decline of remuneration or losing a job as consequences of the virus crises could increase socio-economic disparities, raise unemployment and increase extreme poverty, homelessness, stigma, discrimination and social isolation. Economic crises have been connected to heightened morbidity and mortality, poor nutrition and mental health (Merson et al., 2011; Mucci et al., 2016).

Unemployment and lower salaries will increase stress and lead to physical and mental-health problems (substance abuse, depression and anxiety). In developing countries with prior poverty backgrounds, unemployment will contribute to cases of malnutrition, waterborne infections and other endemic communicable diseases. The subsequent increased sanitary demand on a health system already in financial scarcity creates a continuous circuit of chaos (Merson et al., 2011).

As Durkheim observed, mental health is vulnerable to rapid economic fluctuations (Durkheim, 1897; Wray, Colen and Pescosolido, 2011). Age, gender, race, ethnic cultures and class (income and profession) are acting as determinants of well-being, stimulating or preventing access to medical facilities. They shape the lived experience of illness, both within and outside the health-care system. There is no limit in which an adverse economic conjuncture could worsen the physical and psychological fitness of people.

The COVID-19 pandemic is the first universal health crisis in modern history, and its consequences on the world economies and global mental health are only hypotheses at this point. Health managers should have the vision to plan and strengthen the medical organisation for the economic backlash that will hit the market in the near future. Local societies are already under stress from the emergency, and they will face a financial burden soon. It is the role of health-service leaders to prepare the road to prevent a major collapse in the world population's mental health. Managers should plan for extreme budget constraints, decreased human well-being, increased hospitalisation, political pressures, unstable social structure and a general reduction of health assets in the national health system.

In conclusion, global governance should be adapted to offer a more integrative approach to face a sanitary crisis. The challenges of globalisation impact worldwide quality of life, thereby increasing the probability of pandemic outbreak, and leaders should adopt preventive policies that could foster holistic well-being. The transformational process created by COVID-19 will change the relationship between stakeholders and the perception of the medical system in the population.

A positive leader has to build trust and share a clear vision using the data collected to foresee and prevent a health crisis. There are no two people that have the same set of values and the same moral compasses, and individuals will react to this crisis in different ways. Nevertheless, the health-care managers and national leaders could benefit from the observation of social scientists to develop an appropriate plan with the goal to anticipate problems and tensions in the civil society. This attitude will lead to a better compliance ratio among the population, increasing health policies' efficacy and efficient utilisation of resources.

The head managers of public health should act as role models for their stakeholders (the national community), influencing them to take the right measures with a continuous process of transparency and managing expectations accordingly to realistic output based on quality standard.

Conclusion

Our findings seem to support the critical aspect that mental elements play during the COVID-19 pandemic. Thus, the psychic wellness factor should be accounted for in the public health decision-making process. An appropriate managerial approach could be prepared accordingly, utilising the results from the psychological field.

Psychologists, sociologists, anthropologists, mass communication experts, social researchers, gender and women's specialists, ethnologists and professionals in the social-science areas are essential to provide the technical skills needed to formulate appropriate policies and actions during international health emergencies.

COVID-19 is an opportunity to improve the national health-regulatory model, steering the actual procedures towards a more holistic approach. There is a need for an improved strategy that could offer a comprehensive global vision. Therefore, leaders should develop a plan to supervise business changes to tackle current issues, completing the missing information with reliable data from social-science professionals. Supervisors should set organisational goals and track records of success and failure in implementing consultants and experts. Following the Henri Fayol model, specialisation is an essential feature in scientific management as well as the division of work. Thus, it makes sense that competencies in the human field are integrated into the decision-making process.

Public-health managers have the fiduciary duty to protect the safety of communities. Their stakeholders are the individuals that form the nation, and the assets are citizens' quality of life as defined by the WHO constitutional documents (WHO, 1946):

'Health is a state of complete physical, mental and social well-being and not merely the absence of disease or infirmity'.

CONCLUDING REMARKS

IN THIS LAST CHAPTER, WE sum up our work, providing suggestions to improve public-health management during the pandemic. Our observations could be used as a blueprint for managerial conclusions during a virus outbreak and other mass national-health emergencies.

Our paper aimed to underline the importance of psychological elements during the COVID-19 crisis, showing the risk of inefficient managerial choices when these factors are not taken into account.

Decision-makers have to consider mental-health principles in the creation of public-health policies with a twofold point of view:

1. How does psychological process impact the stakeholders and the population?

2. Which preventive measure should be enforced in order to reduce the psychological distress in the population?

The first point could be addressed by creating two advisory subgroups in the decision-making process: one whose specific goal is to appraise whether some psychological aspect affected the result and another that will analyse the psychosocial consequences of the final resolution, forecasting behaviours of the population. These subgroups should be composed of well-recognised experts in the social-science fields.

The second point should consider the repercussions on citizens' mental health and well-being, and prepare the medical system to cope with the possibility of increasing demand. Thus, appropriate capabilities, both financial and logistical, should be planned in time. Underinvestment in mental health should be promptly corrected. Adequate personnel should be already identified in case of subsequent needs. Suitable training should be established to supply the technical resources required in case of a long-term surge in mental-health conditions.

In the meantime, the current and future stressor should be addressed. As an example, uncertainty and lack of information represent major stressors. Thus, appropriate media diffusion should be offered with accurate news. Practical documentation should be disseminated, and religious and civil leaders should be involved in the distribution of detailed advice and accurate information. According to the needs of the general population, performing target interventions could prevent additional costs for the health sector.

Particular attention should be paid to the frontline workers, individuals with a pre-existing medical condition, children, college students and people in social isolation and financial distress. Special mental-health training should be mandatory for medical personnel, with a double goal to raise awareness among healthcare providers about their own mental well-being and increase the capacity to detect suffering in patients and the general population.

A holistic approach to national programmes is essential to prepare a good plan. Policies should be organised through committees that include experts in the mental-health field and social sciences. Psychosocial support should be strengthened, and programmes to increase social cohesion and respect sanitary measures should be implemented.

Mental-health policies should be reformed and systems should be reorganised, adapting them to the new situation and in prescience of growing need for psychiatric and psychological services. This scheduling has to be carefully prepared in a timely manner, as the creations and allocations of human resources require long educational studies.

Finally, adequate funding should be allocated to promote research on the pandemic impact on mental well-being. Data should be made publicly available for the scientific community, the stakeholders and decision-makers.

In case no preventive measures are taken and the health system is not ready to react to the increasing demand for psychic services, there is a real possibility of the collapse of hospitals and other public-health structures. With the COVID-19 virus, we had an obvious example of the critical position healthcare facilities occupy because of a lack of prescience and inadequate planning.

Like many other works produced during this pandemic, our work suggests the necessity of a powerful reaction of public-health managers to prevent a future crisis, this time related to mental-health struggles. There is enough documentation to understand the severity of the population's well-being, with particular attention to youngsters. This historic moment is creating a Covid-generation that will become the forthcoming population of the world. There is an urgency to be sure that adequate resources are prepared in time, before there is a need to deal with a generation affected by PTSD and other psychiatric disorders. Just as cautionary tales, we would remind that a generation affected by mental-health burdens is economically non-productive; hence, there is the risk that future citizens cannot create the means and resources needed to take care of themselves.

Forecast problems mean to forewarn and prepare the vanguard to defend against complex issues.

Additionally, the rational assessment of the quarantine and the limitations of movement should be evaluated considering the impact on citizens' psychological well-being. Governmental health leaders opted to use restriction of freedom, basing their decisions on three parameters: epidemiologist recommendations, economic implications and political consequences. There is a clear void in taking into account the immediate costs on mental fitness and the long-lasting effects on mental and physical healthiness. Health management should have a long-term vision and move from a reactive managerial process to a more proactive approach. Ongoing studies show that quarantine and other actions decided in urgency and haste could have a high cost for the youngest members of the population. From a strategic perspective, the reactive solutions could have the worst consequences in the foreseeable future, both from a psychological and a social perspective.

The public-health managers could find difficulties in allocating the budget to prevent a mental-health crisis. From an economic point of view, it makes more sense to provide adequate resources now to fund the structure and policies than to react to an ongoing mental-health crisis in the future. The future costs to minister to a considerable part of the population affected by psychiatric disorders who cannot be productive are higher than the current investment in their well-being. Besides, a cost distributed through the years has a minor impact on the national economies than funding allocated due to urgency.

The ethical aspect is an essential point that public-health managers should raise in allocating and requesting the means needed to plan. Managers have the responsibility to allocate the required capacities today in order to avoid the younger generation's suffering and avert a social crisis. The difficulty in meeting a realistic moral goal is correlated with the notion that healthcare is a fundamental right, but it also is a business; thus, public-health managers have the complicated role to decide when the ethical implications overcome the economic challenges in the broader vision of long-term management of national resources.

In conclusion, there is an opportunity to learn some lessons from this crisis. COVID-19 pandemic is a moment that should not be wasted, but used instead to improve our managerial practice, develop a more holistic approach to policymaking and create a hub of experience for the future health crisis. World leaders lost an incredible amount of knowledge and understanding during and immediately following the Ebola outbreak. We should not let the COVID-19 challenge be solved with no gained insight, instead using this historical occasion to implement best practices in national public-health management.

BIBLIOGRAPHY

Ahmed, M. Z. et al. (2020). 'Epidemic of COVID-19 in China and associated Psychological Problems'. Asian Journal of Psychiatry, 51. doi:10.1016/j.ajp.2020.102092.

Barari, S. et al. (2020). 'Evaluating COVID-19 public health messaging in Italy: Self-reported compliance and growing mental health concerns'. medRxiv. doi:10.1101/2020.03.27.20042820.

Benson, B. (2016). Cognitive bias cheat sheet. Because thinking is hard. Available at: https://medium.com/better-humans/cognitive-bias-cheat-sheet-55a472476b18 (Accessed: 25 January 2021).

Birch, S. A. J. et al. (2017). 'A "curse of knowledge" in the absence of knowledge? People misattribute fluency when judging how common knowledge is among their peers'. Cognition. doi:10.1016/j.cognition.2017.04.015.

Bluestone, H. (1998). 'Social Support and Psychiatric Disorder: Research Findings and Guidelines for Clinical Practice'. American Journal of Psychiatry, 155(7), 988a–989. doi:10.1176/ajp.155.7.988a.

Bonanno, G. A. (2004). 'Loss, Trauma, and Human Resilience: Have We Underestimated the Human Capacity to Thrive after Extremely Aversive Events?' American Psychologist, 20–28. doi:10.1037/0003-066X.59.1.20.

Bonanno, G. A., and Diminich, E. D. (2013). 'Annual research review: Positive adjustment to adversity—Trajectories of minimal-impact resilience and emergent resilience'. Journal of Child Psychology and Psychiatry and Allied Disciplines. 378–401. doi:10.1111/jcpp.12021.

Bonardi, J.-P. et al. (2020). Fast and Local: How Did Lockdown Policies Affect the Spread and Severity of COVID-19? Available at: https://cepr.org/sites/default/files/news/CovidEconomics23.pdf (Accessed: 17 January 2021).

Brodeur, A. et al. (2020). COVID-19, Lockdowns and Well-Being: Evidence from Google Trends. Available at: www.iza.org (Accessed: 29 September 2020).

Brooks, S. K. et al. (2020). 'Rapid Review The psychological impact of quarantine and how to reduce it: rapid review of the evidence'. The Lancet, 395. doi:10.1016/S0140-6736(20) 30460-8.

Carr, C. P. et al. (2013). 'The Role of Early Life Stress in Adult Psychiatric Disorders'. The Journal of Nervous and Mental Disease, 201(12), 1007–1020. doi:10.1097/NMD.0000000000000049.

Center for Family Strengthening Five Protective Factors | cfsslo (2021). Available at: https://cfsslo.org/five-protective-factors/ (Accessed: 2 February 2021).

Cherry, K. E. et al. (2018). 'Spirituality, Humor, and Resilience After Natural and Technological Disasters'. Journal of Nursing Scholarship, 50(5), 492–501. doi:10.1111/jnu.12400.

Cibrian-Llanderal, T., Melgarejo-Gutierrez, M. and Hernandez-Baltazar, D. (2018). 'Stress and Cognition: Psychological Basis and Support Resources'. Health and Academic Achievement. doi:10.5772/intechopen.72566.

Diagnostic and Statistical Manual of DSM-5 TM (2013).

Diamond, A. (2013). 'Executive functions'. Annual Review of Psychology. 135–168. doi:10.1146/annurev-psych-113011-143750.

Dillard, J. P. and Shen, L. (2005). 'On the nature of reactance and its role in persuasive health communication'. Communication Monographs. doi:10.1080/03637750500111815.

Drury, J. (2020). 'Recent developments in the psychology of crowds and collective behaviour'. Current Opinion in Psychology. 12–16. doi:10.1016/j.copsyc.2020.02.005.

Drury, J. et al. (2019). 'Facilitating collective psychosocial resilience in the public in emergencies: Twelve recommendations based on the social identity approach'. Frontiers in Public Health. doi:10.3389/fpubh.2019.00141.

Drury, J. and Reicher, S. D. (2018). 'The conservative crowd? How participation in collective events transforms participants' understandings of collective action'. The Psychology of Radical Social Change: From Rage to Revolution (pp. 11–28). Cambridge University Press. doi:10.1017/9781108377461.003.

Durkheim, E. (1897). On Suicide. Available at: https://www.bookdepository. com/On-Suicide-Emile-Durkheim/9780140449679 (Accessed: 2 February 2021).

Fekih-Romdhane, F. et al. (2020). 'Psychological impact of the Pandemic COVID-19 Outbreak Among Medical Residents in Tunisia'. Asian Journal of Psychiatry. doi:10.1016/j.ajp.2020.102349.

Furnham, A. and Boo, H. C. (2011). 'A literature review of the anchoring effect'. Journal of Socio-Economics. doi:10.1016/j.socec.2010.10.008.

Gadek-Michalska, A. et al. (2013). 'Cytokines, prostaglandins and nitric oxide in the regulation of stress-response systems'. Pharmacological Reports, 65(6), 1655–1662. doi:10.1016/S1734-1140(13) 71527-5.

Gao, J. et al. (2020). 'Mental health problems and social media exposure during COVID-19 outbreak'. PLoS ONE, 15(4). doi:10.1371/journal. pone.0231924.

Geller, J. L. and Warner, R. (1997). 'Social Support and Psychiatric Disorder: Research Findings and Guidelines for Clinical Practice'. Psychiatric Services, 48(4), 548. doi:10.1176/ps.48.4.548.

Goyal, K. et al. (2020). 'Fear of COVID 2019: First suicidal case in India!' Asian Journal of Psychiatry. 101989. doi:10.1016/j.ajp.2020.101989.

Grossman, M. (1972), 'On the Concept of Health Capital and the Demand for Health'. Journal of Political Economy. 80(2), 223–255.

Gruber, R. et al. (2020). 'The impact of COVID-19 related school shutdown on sleep in adolescents: a natural experiment'. Sleep Medicine, 76, 33–35. doi:10.1016/j.sleep.2020.09.015.

Hänsel, A. et al. (2010). 'Inflammation as a psychophysiological biomarker in chronic psychosocial stress'. Neuroscience and Biobehavioral Reviews, 115–121. doi:10.1016/j.neubiorev.2009.12.012.

Harris, A. J. L. and Hahn, U. (2011). 'Unrealistic Optimism About Future Life Events: A Cautionary Note'. Psychological Review. doi:10.1037/a0020997.

Haselton, M. G., Nettle, D. and Andrews, P. W. (2015). 'The Evolution of Cognitive Bias'. The Handbook of Evolutionary Psychology. doi:10.1002/9780470939376.ch25.

Heilman, R. M. et al. (2010). 'Emotion Regulation and Decision Making Under Risk and Uncertainty'. Emotion, 10(2), 257–265. doi:10.1037/a0018489.

Heim, C. and Nemeroff, C. B. (2001). 'The role of childhood trauma in the neurobiology of mood and anxiety disorders: Preclinical and clinical studies'. Biological Psychiatry. 1023–1039. doi:10.1016/S0006-3223(01) 01157-X.

Huebener, M. et al. (2020). Parental Well-Being in Times of COVID-19 in Germany. Available at: www.RePEc.org (Accessed: 30 September 2020).

Hueston, C. M. and Deak, T. (2014). 'The inflamed axis: The interaction between stress, hormones, and the expression of inflammatory-related genes within key structures comprising the hypothalamic-pituitary-adrenal axis'. Physiology and Behavior, 124, 77–91. doi:10.1016/j.physbeh.2013.10.035.

Ing, E. B. et al. (2020). 'Physician deaths from corona virus (COVID-19) disease'. Occupational Medicine, 70(5), 370–374. doi:10.1093/occmed/kqaa088.

Irwin, M. (2002). 'Effects of sleep and sleep loss on immunity and cytokines'. Brain, Behavior, and Immunity. doi:10.1016/S0889-1591(02) 00003-X.

Johnson, D. K. (2017). 'Confirmation bias'. Bad Arguments: 50 Common Fallacies and How to Avoid Them. doi:10.1002/9781119165811.ch73.

Jost, J. T., Banaji, M. R. and Nosek, B. A. (2004). 'A decade of system justification theory: Accumulated evidence of conscious and unconscious bolstering of the status quo'. Political Psychology. doi:10.1111/j.1467-9221.2004.00402.x.

Kahneman, D. (2014). Thinking, Fast and Slow. Farrar, Straus and Giroux.

Kang, L. et al. (2020). 'The mental health of medical workers in Wuhan, China dealing with the 2019 novel coronavirus'. The Lancet Psychiatry. e14. doi:10.1016/S2215-0366(20) 30047-X.

Kim, B. and Zhao, Y. (2020). 'Psychological Suffering Owing to Lockdown or Fear of Infection? Evidence from the COVID-19 Outbreak in China'. Discussion Paper Series. Available at: https://ideas.repec.org/p/iek/wpaper/2008.html (Accessed: 29 September 2020).

Kinsey, M. J. et al. (2019). 'Cognitive Biases Within Decision Making During Fire Evacuations'. Fire Technology (pp. 465–485). Springer doi:10.1007/s10694-018-0708-0.

Kurzweil, R. (2004). 'The Law of Accelerating Returns'. Alan Turing: Life and Legacy of a Great Thinker. doi:10.1007/978-3-662-05642-4_16.

Lange, T., Dimitrov, S. and Born, J. (2010). 'Effects of sleep and circadian rhythm on the human immune system: Annals of the New York Academy of Sciences'. Annals of the New York Academy of Sciences (pp. 48–59). Blackwell Publishing Inc. doi:10.1111/j.1749-6632.2009.05300.x.

Lehmann, M. et al. (2015). 'Ebola and psychological stress of health care professionals'. Emerging Infectious Diseases. Centers for Disease Control and Prevention (CDC), 913–914. doi:10.3201/eid2105.141988.

Li, Q. et al. (2020). 'Early Transmission Dynamics in Wuhan, China, of Novel Coronavirus–Infected Pneumonia'. New England Journal of Medicine, 382(13), 1199–1207. doi:10.1056/NEJMoa2001316.

McFarlane, A. C. (1992). 'Avoidance and intrusion in posttraumatic stress disorder'. Journal of Nervous and Mental Disease, 180(7), 439–445. doi:10.1097/00005053-199207000-00006.

McFarlane, A. C. (2007). 'Stress-related musculoskeletal pain'. Best Practice and Research: Clinical Rheumatology. 549–565. doi:10.1016/j.berh.2007.03.008.

McFarlane, A. C. (2010). 'The long-term costs of traumatic stress: Intertwined physical and psychological consequences'. World Psychiatry, 9(1), 3–10. doi:10.1002/j.2051-5545.2010.tb00254.x.

Merson, M. H. et al. (2011). Global Health: Diseases, Programs, Systems, and Policies, Third Edition. London: Jones & Bartlett Learning.

Mesurado, B., Vidal, E. M. and Mestre, A. L. (2018). 'Negative emotions and behaviour: The role of regulatory emotional self-efficacy'. Journal of Adolescence, 64, 62–71. doi:10.1016/j.adolescence.2018.01.007.

Miyake, A. et al. (2000). 'The Unity and Diversity of Executive Functions and Their Contributions to Complex "Frontal Lobe" Tasks: A Latent Variable Analysis'. Cognitive Psychology, 41(1), 49–100. doi:10.1006/cogp.1999.0734.

Mrazek, P. J. and Haggerty, R. J. (1994). 'Risk and Protective Factors for the Onset of Mental Disorders'. Available at: https://www.ncbi.nlm.nih.gov/ books/NBK236306/ (Accessed: 2 February 2021).

Moussaïd, M. et al. (2016). 'Crowd behaviour during high-stress evacuations in an immersive virtual environment'. Journal of the Royal Society Interface, 13(122). doi:10.1098/rsif.2016.0414.

Mucci, N. et al. (2016). 'The correlation between stress and economic crisis: A systematic review'. Neuropsychiatric Disease and Treatment (pp. 983–993). Dove Medical Press Ltd. doi:10.2147/NDT.S98525.

Newall, N. E. G. et al. (2013). 'Consequences of loneliness on physical activity and mortality in older adults and the power of positive emotions'. Health Psychology, 32(8), 921–924. doi:10.1037/a0029413.

Nickerson, R. S. (1998). 'Confirmation bias: A ubiquitous phenomenon in many guises'. Review of General Psychology. doi:10.1037/1089-2680.2.2.175.

Omer, H. and Alon, N. (1994). 'The continuity principle: A unified approach to disaster and trauma'. American Journal of Community Psychology. doi:10.1007/BF02506866.

Parra-Uribe, I. et al. (2017). 'Risk of re-attempts and suicide death after a suicide attempt: A survival analysis'. BMC Psychiatry, 17(1), 163. doi:10.1186/ s12888-017-1317-z.

Paules, C. I., Marston, H. D. and Fauci, A. S. (2020). 'Coronavirus Infections— More Than Just the Common Cold'. JAMA—Journal of the American Medical Association,707–708. doi:10.1001/jama.2020.0757.

Paykel, E. S. (1978). 'Contribution of life events to causation of psychiatric illness'.Psychological Medicine, 8(2), 245–253. doi:10.1017/S003329170001429X.

Pennycook, G. et al. (2017). 'Dunning–Kruger effects in reasoning: Theoretical implications of the failure to recognize incompetence' Psychonomic Bulletin and Review. doi:10.3758/s13423-017-1242-7.

Prasad, V. and Jena, A. B. (2014). 'The Peltzman effect and compensatory markers in medicine'. Healthcare. doi:10.1016/j.hjdsi.2014.05.002.

Pronin, E. (2007). 'Perception and misperception of bias in human judgment'. Trends in Cognitive Sciences. doi:10.1016/j.tics.2006.11.001.

Pronin, E., Gilovich, T. and Ross, L. (2004). 'Objectivity in the eye of the beholder: Divergent perceptions of bias in self versus others'. Psychological Review. doi:10.1037/0033-295X.111.3.781.

Quick, J. D. (1987). 'Health consequences of stress'. Journal of Organizational Behavior Management, 8(2), 19–36. doi:10.1300/J075v08n02_03.

Ren, Y. et al. (2020). 'Public mental health under the long-term influence of COVID-19 in China: Geographical and temporal distribution'. Journal of Affective Disorders, 277, 893–900. doi:10.1016/j.jad.2020.08.045.

Riboni, F. V. and Belzung, C. (2017). 'Stress and psychiatric disorders: from categorical to dimensional approaches'. Current Opinion in Behavioral Sciences, 72–77. doi:10.1016/j.cobeha.2016.12.011.

Saladino, V., Algeri, D. and Auriemma, V. (2020). 'The Psychological and Social Impact of COVID-19: New Perspectives of Well-Being'. Frontiers in Psychology, 11, 2550. doi:10.3389/fpsyg.2020.577684.

Salvatori, G. (2020). Italian doctor dies of coronavirus after working without gloves due to shortage. Euronews. Available at: https://www.euronews.com/2020/03/18/italian-doctor-dies-of-coronavirus-after-working-without-gloves-due-to-shortage (Accessed: 3 February 2021).

Schmitt, A. et al. (2014). 'The impact of environmental factors in severe psychiatric disorders'. Frontiers in Neuroscience, 19. doi:10.3389/fnins.2014.00019.

Schnurr, P. P., and Green, B. L. (2005). 'Trauma and health: Physical health consequences of exposure to extreme stress'. American Psychological Association. doi:10.1037/10723-000.

Schwartz, N. G. et al. (2020). 'Adolescent with COVID-19 as the Source of an Outbreak at a 3-Week Family Gathering — Four States, June–July 2020'. Morbidity and Mortality Weekly Report, 69(40), 1457–1459. doi:10.15585/ mmwr.mm6940e2.

Segerstrom, S. C. and Miller, G. E. (2004). 'Psychological stress and the human immune system: A meta-analytic study of 30 years of inquiry'. Psychological Bulletin, 130(4), 601–630. doi:10.1037/0033-2909.130.4.601.

Shields, G. S. et al. (2016). 'The effect of negative affect on cognition: Anxiety, not anger, impairs executive function'. Emotion, 16(6), 792–797. doi:10.1037/ emo0000151.

Sunstein, C. R. (2003). 'Terrorism and Probability Neglect'. Journal of Risk and Uncertainty. doi:10.1023/A:1024111006336.

Torrance, E. P. and Brehm, J. W. (1968). 'A Theory of Psychological Reactance'. The American Journal of Psychology. doi:10.2307/1420824.

Werner, E. E. (1993). 'Risk, resilience, and recovery: Perspectives from the Kauai Longitudinal Study'. Development and Psychopathology, 5(4), 503– 515. doi:10.1017/S095457940000612X.

Werner, E. E. (2014). 'High-risk children in young adulthood: A longitudinal study from birth to 32 years'. Risks and Problem Behaviors in Adolescence (pp. 76–86). Taylor and Francis. Available at: https://pubmed.ncbi.nlm.nih. gov/2467566/ (Accessed: 2 February 2021).

Werner, E. E. and Smith, R. S. (1992). Overcoming the Odds. Cornell University Press. doi:10.7591/9781501711992.

Wilke, A. and Mata, R. (2012). 'Cognitive bias'. Encyclopedia of Human Behavior: Second Edition. doi:10.1016/B978-0-12-375000-6.00094-X.

Wray, M., Colen, C. and Pescosolido, B. (2011). 'The sociology of suicide'. Annual Review of Sociology, 37, 505–528. doi:10.1146/ annurev-soc-081309-150058.

Yang, Xiao et al. (2020). 'Social support and clinical improvement in COVID-19 positive patients in China'. Nursing Outlook. doi:10.1016/j. outlook.2020.08.008.

Yeager, D. S., Dahl, R. E. and Dweck, C. S. (2018). 'Why interventions to influence adolescent behavior often fail but could succeed'. Perspectives on Psychological Science, 13(1), 101–122. doi:10.1177/1745691617722620.

WHO. (1946). Constitution of the World Health Organization. Available at: https://www.who.int/governance/eb/who_constitution_en.pdf (Accessed: 28 September 2020).

Zhou, Y. et al. (2020). 'The prevalence and risk factors of psychological disturbances of frontline medical staff in china under the COVID-19 epidemic: Workload should be concerned'. Journal of Affective Disorders, 277, 510–514. doi:10.1016/j.jad.2020.08.059.

APPENDIX

sources

SOURCE	NATION
Cesifo	German
The Institute of Economic Research	Korea
Asian Journal of Psychiatry	Netherlands
Biological Psychiatry	Netherlands
Cognition	Netherlands
Fire Technology	Netherlands
Journal of Affective Disorders	Netherlands
Journal of Risk and Uncertainty	Netherlands
Journal of Socio-Economics	Netherlands
Sleep Medicine	Netherlands
Trends in Cognitive Sciences	Netherlands
Best Practice and Research: Clinical Rheumatology	United Kingdom
Cambridge University Press	United Kingdom
Communication Monographs	United Kingdom
Current Opinion in Psychology	United Kingdom
Encyclopedia of Human Behavior	United Kingdom
Journal of Affective Disorders	United Kingdom
Journal of Nursing Scholarship	United Kingdom
Neuroscience and Biobehavioral Reviews	United Kingdom

Political Psychology	United Kingdom
Psychological Medicine	United Kingdom
The Lancet	United Kingdom
The Lancet Psychiatry	United Kingdom
American Journal of Community Psychology	United States
American Psychologist	United States
Annals of the New York Academy of Sciences	United States
Brain, Behavior, and Immunity	United States
Diagnostic and Statistical Manual of DSM-5	United States
Emerging Infectious Diseases. Centers for Disease Control and Prevention (CDC)	United States
JAMA—Journal of the American Medical Association.	United States
Journal of Child Psychology and Psychiatry	United States
Journal of Nervous and Mental Disease	United States
Journal of Nursing Scholarship	United States
MedRxiv	United States
MMWR. Morbidity and Mortality Weekly Report	United States
New England Journal of Medicine	United States
Nursing Outlook	United States
Perspectives on Psychological Science	United States
PLoS ONE	United States
Psychiatric Services	United States
Psychological Bulletin	United States
Psychological Review	United States
Psychological Review	United States

Psychonomic Bulletin and Review	United States
Review of General Psychology	United States
Science Direct	United States
Sleep Medicine	United States
The American Journal of Psychology	United States
The Handbook of Evolutionary Psychology	United States
World Psychiatry	United States

stressors

Isolation due to quarantine	The COVID-19 disease
Wearing protective equipment	Death of loved ones
Difficulties in providing the basic needs	Misinformation
Financial distress	Too much information
Incertitude for the future	Shortage of health care
Digital overconsumption	Seclusion
Social distancing	Reduced freedom of movement
Impossible to reach family	Overwhelming media exposure

consequences

Physical	Emotional	Behavioural	Cognitive	Psychiatric
Back pain	Anger	Aggressiveness	Circular thoughts	Depression
Chest pains	Distrust	Diffusion of fake news	Denial	Anxiety disorder
Digestive problems	Emptiness or hopelessness	Drug abuse	Impaired cognitive functions	Burnout
Dizziness	Fear	Excessive attention to symptoms	Impaired executive function	CPTSD
Headaches	Guilt	Increase in psychotropic medication	Misjudgement	Paranoia
High blood pressure	Helplessness	Increased screen time	Lack of focus	Dissociative symptoms
High cholesterol	Lower self-esteem	Isolation	Loss of memory	Personality disorders
Low energy	Melancholy	Restlessness	Nightmares	PTSD
Low human immune system	Mood fluctuations	Self-harm	Rumination	
Low sex drive	Rage	Suicide	Burnout	
Sleep deprivation	Sadness	Violence	Stress	

protective factors

Appropriate diet	Regular physical activity
Availability of mental health services	Religious community
Emotional competence	Strong attachments (parent–child)
Expressing gratitude	Strong social network
Genetic factors	Supportive family
Meditation and breathing exercises	Supportive peers
Parental resilience	Using grounding techniques
Pet therapy	Volunteering

The self-perception of one's knowledge of social sciences inversely correlates with one's objective knowledge of social sciences.